GANGL

VANISHED:
THE LIFE & DISAPPEARANCE OF
JIMMY HOFFA

WILLIAM HRYB

Copyright 2013 by William Hryb
All Rights Reserved

No part of this book may be reproduced, stored in a
retrieval system, or transmitted in any form, by any
means, including mechanical, electronic photocopying,
recording or otherwise, without the prior written permission of the publisher, except by a reviewer who wishes to
quote brief passages in connection with a review written
for inclusion in a magazine, newspaper or broadcast.

Requests for permission should be directed to:
strategicmediabooks@gmail.com,
or mailed to:
Permissions, Strategic Media Inc.
782 Wofford St., Rock Hill, SC 29730.

13-digit ISBN 978-0985-2440-8-8
10-digit ISBN 0-9852440-8-9

ACKNOWLEDGEMENTS

This book would not have been possible without the support and encouragement from my amazing wife Lee Hryb... thank you Lone. My children, Kaiti, Christeann and David for their wonderful enthusiasm for this project. To my dear mother and aunt, and of course my brothers Mihail and Lajo who were eager for me to complete this journey.

Thank you to John Wewiora, who was responsible for fueling my ego in this effort and Jace Cella, for his genuine interest in Jimmy Hoffa.

A special thank you to Ron Chepesiuk for his assistance with the book and to Elle Andra-Warner for her advice and guidance.

My sincere gratitude to Barbara Casey for her exceptional help with this book...thank you...

Last but not least, to my father, close friends Jake and Dave who are not here, but would have celebrated the book's publication with gusto.

CONTENTS

WILLIAM HRYB

PROLOGUE

W hen James Riddle Hoffa was ordered to report to Lewisburg Federal Prison in March of 1967, his life was in tatters. A thirteen-year prison sentence awaited him. From 1957 to 1959, Robert Kennedy relentlessly pursued Jimmy Hoffa: a man reputed to be one of the most powerful figures in North America. Spearheaded by the young lawyer, Robert Kennedy, Hoffa became the target of congressional hearings into organized crime within the U.S. labor movement.

Watched by millions, the McClellan hearings exposed the public to a fascinating look at corruption in the Teamsters Union at its highest levels. Jimmy Hoffa, president of the Teamsters, was front and center to investigations that eventually brought him down.

Ten months into the extraordinary hearings, Americans awoke to sensational headlines. On November 14, 1957, in a small village in upstate New York, Mob bosses from all over the country—Carlo Gambino, Joe Bonanno, Vito Genovese, Joe Profaci, Cuba Mob boss Santo Traffi-cante, and future Gambino boss Paul Castellano, for example—were nabbed by Sergeant Edgar D. Croswell as the Mafia elite gathered to organize and sort out a bloody war of succession. The meeting was held at the sprawling estate of Mobster Joseph "Joe the Barber" in Apalachin, New York, to discuss various topics including loan sharking, narcotics trafficking and gambling, along with dividing the illegal operations once controlled by the late Albert Anastasia. Over one hundred Mafioso from the United States, Canada and Italy were at the Mob conference adding credence to the Mafia's strength in numbers. For decades, FBI Director J. Edgar Hoover denied the existence of the Mafia, but after the sensational discovery at Apalachin, Hoover was forced to admit that the Mafia was real.

Thirty-one-year-old Robert Kennedy had no illusions about the revelations and recognized the importance of the Mob summit. When his brother John Fitzgerald Kennedy became the president, Robert Kennedy launched a campaign to break the back of the Mob, engaging Jimmy Hoffa in a boiling turf battle. The Mob summit not only confirmed the existence of the American Mafia, but it also reaffirmed the notion that John R. McClellan hearings overlapped the dramatic discovery, proving to authorities and the American public that organized crime was flourishing in the United States. The disclosure humiliated J. Edgar Hoover who finally had to admit that the Mafia was no fantasy.

CHAPTER ONE

THE BEGINNING OF THE END

With the McClellan hearings spearheaded by Robert Kennedy came a daily dose of shocking disclosures that organized crime had crept into the very inner circles of the labor movement. The hearings conducted between 1957 and 1959 had a carnival-like atmosphere, where prosecutors dissected every word of suspected persons who had ties to organized crime and the underworld. Jimmy Hoffa and Robert Kennedy would become bitter enemies. The blood feud remained until the day Robert Kennedy was shot and mortally wounded after he had won the California Democratic primary in 1968. At the time of Robert Kennedy's death, Jimmy Hoffa was in prison for jury tampering, fraud and conspiracy.

When he learned of Kennedy's death, condolences were not on his mind. Robert Kennedy's brother, John F. Kennedy, his arch-enemy, had been assassinated in Dallas five years earlier.

Hoffa finally had the Kennedys off his back.

Just weeks after John F. Kennedy was inaugurated President of the United States in 1961, one of his first cabinet appointments was his brother, Robert Kennedy, as attorney general. During the McClellan hearings Bobby Kennedy went after Hoffa like a blood hound but with little tangible success in bringing down the Teamster leader.

Now Kennedy had the full power of his office to bring Hoffa down and put him away in prison for a very long time. "We know that it is the law which enables men to live together, that creates order out of chaos. We know that the law is the glue that holds civilization together. And we know that if one man's rights are denied, the rights of the others are endangered," said Robert F. Kennedy in 1961, referring to one of the most powerful labor leaders in U.S. history.

Jimmy Hoffa's life reads like a Shakespearean play.

Standing no more than 5'6", Hoffa's stature belied his tenacity and determination. He would get his way by sometimes using brute force, and that character trait catapulted him onto the national scene as a fierce advocate for Teamsters' rights. Accusations that Hoffa and the International Brotherhood of Teamsters were tied to organized crime eventually caught the attention of the US Department of Justice, which instigated a relentless pursuit. With the notoriety and undisputed power Jimmy Hoffa held, the perception that the Union was controlled by organized crime was gaining strength. As a result, the McClellan Committee opened senate hearings on February 26, 1957, to investigate corruption, criminal infiltration, and illegal activities in the nation's labor unions, particularly the Teamsters.

Chaired by Democrat John McClellan, the committee included John F. Kennedy and Barry Goldwater, along with Robert Kennedy as chief counsel. The committee's investigation focused on the International Brotherhood of Teamsters, Teamsters' president Dave Beck, and Beck's successor Jimmy Hoffa. In televised hearings viewed by over 1.2 million households daily, the committee detailed the Teamsters' misuse of Union funds and ties to labor racketeers and organized crime. The inquiry led to the conviction of over twenty individuals, including Beck, but failed to convict Hoffa, making him look invincible. As a result of Dave Beck's conviction, the AFL/CIO (American Federation of Labor and Congress of Industrial Organization) expelled the Teamsters from their ranks.

More than 1,500 witnesses were called to testify at the hearings, uncovering a stupefying account on how labor leaders, management, public officials, and the Mafia worked to swindle and threaten rank-and-file Union members. The efforts of the committee initiated the Labor-Management Reporting and Disclosure Act of 1959, establishing for the first time close regulation of Unions by the federal government. The rigid law created requirements for Union elections and for the filing of annual financial reports to the Labor Department, banned convicted felons from holding Union office and instituted Union members' rights against coercive labor practices. The days of unregulated Union practices were over.

Labor racketeering was the prime target for federal investigators with Jimmy Hoffa the number one suspect. Hounded relentlessly by federal authorities, Hoffa seemed untouchable. Most of the rank and file respected Hoffa and forgave his excesses. One Union member recalled, "Hoffa did steal from us but he also gave us a hell of a lot." Early in his career, Hoffa's reputation as a tough negotiator at the bargaining table and even tougher in a street brawl ingratiated him with Union members. He was adept at rousing support from the rank and file to consolidate his power base. With that strength, Hoffa shifted far beyond his stronghold in Detroit's Local 299 and the area's Joint Council of Teamsters. He was now able to garner enough support to take control of the Central and Southern States Conference, bringing him to national recognition. Often violent and ruthless, Hoffa wasn't shy in developing a close relationship with underworld individuals, which gave him the muscle he needed. At its height, the Teamsters Union under Jimmy Hoffa became so powerful it was able to control the wages and working conditions of the entire trucking industry. A strike called by Hoffa had the potential to shut down the transportation system and cripple the North American economy. Jimmy Hoffa was at the pinnacle of his game.

Despite Jimmy Hoffa's remarkable rise in the Teamsters, the McClellan Committee hearings would prove to be Hoffa's eventual downfall. From the onset of the two-and-a-half years of testimony, Robert Kennedy and Jimmy Hoffa went at it like street fighters. Hoffa and other

Union leaders were called to testify about ties to the underworld. Kennedy was able to uncover evidence of payoffs and racketeering and exposed how Unions bought, sold, and, on occasion, stole to control Unions. Kennedy also showed what happened to the individuals who challenged Hoffa. In 1960, John F. Kennedy was elected president in one of the closest elections in U.S. history, defeating Richard M. Nixon. The Kennedys now had the power to ratchet up the heat on corrupt labor unions, particularly the Teamsters and Jimmy Hoffa. Prior to JFK's election, the McClellan hearings succeeded in bringing the ills of Union activities to the forefront, but did little to put Hoffa behind bars.

Soon after his inauguration, JFK appointed his brother, Robert Kennedy, attorney general giving him unlimited authority to continue his crusade against Hoffa. In October 1963, Joseph Valachi, a low-ranking member of the New York based Genovese crime family, testified on the inner workings of the *La Cosa Nostra,* proving the existence of the American Mafia as well as naming members and the major crime families. In 1964, one year after JFK's assassination, charges against Hoffa stuck, and in 1967, after exhausting his appeals, Hoffa was ordered to report to federal prison at Lewisburg, Pennsylvania.

The man behind Hoffa's conviction was Edward Grady Parton, a Teamster who was awaiting trial for a variety of crimes. Parton saw an opportunity to save himself and offered to assist the Justice Department to convict the Teamster boss for jury tampering. A business manager for Teamsters Local 5 in Baton Rouge, Louisiana, for thirty years, Parton testified that Hoffa offered him

$20,000 to fix the jury at his 1962 trial in which he faced charges of taking kickbacks from a trucking company. Before he left for Lewisburg Prison, Hoffa gave his right-hand man, Frank Fitzsimmons, the responsibility of care-taker boss until his release. The understanding was that Hoffa would still run the Union from jail and Fitzsim-mons would take care of day-to-day Union business. Late in 1971, in a surprise move, President Richard M. Nixon commuted Hoffa's sentence after serving nearly five years of a thirteen-year prison term. Hoffa's release was greeted with excitement, but when he found out there was a string attached, Hoffa exploded. The stipulation of the release, that he could not engage in Union activities until 1980, enraged Hoffa. The Union boss was not used to being double-crossed and he did not like it. He tried to reclaim the Union presidency but Fitzsimmons refused to step aside and told Hoffa to "get lost." The secret deal be-tween Fitzsimmons and Nixon's advisors gave them what they wanted—the Union leadership for Fitzsimmons, and support by the Teamsters for Nixon's re-election cam-paign in 1972. The Mob was happy, too—they had Fitz-simmons in their back pocket with access to millions of dollars in pension funds.

CHAPTER TWO

HOFFA'S EARLY LIFE

James Riddle Hoffa was born on Valentine's Day, February 14, 1913, in the poor mining town of Brazil, Clay County, Indiana, 60 miles west of Indianapolis. Hoffa was the third of four children born to a Pennsylvania Dutch coal miner named John Cleveland Hoffa and an Irish immigrant mother named Viola Riddle. The boy seemed destined for controversy as his family tree revealed a dark chapter on both his paternal and maternal sides.

The Hoffa clan can be traced to Johann Henrich Hoffa who was born December 29, 1739, in Aldingen, Baden-Wurttemberg, Germany, and died of the croup in Reading, Berks County, Pennsylvania, in 1802. The descendants of Hoffa's paternal grandmother, Nancy Jane Asher, migrated to America in the early 1700s. Nancy's lineage goes back three generations to David Asher, born June 12,

1759, in North Carolina. Asher served as a soldier during the American Revolution in 1775. David Asher's grandson, James Asher, Hoffa's first cousin three times removed, elected not to choose sides during the American Civil War eighty-seven years later. Instead, he joined his uncle, Charlie Asher, and a friend, John Newby, in hiding out to avoid fighting in the North-South conflict. A warning by bushwhackers known as the Adams Bunch threatened to kill them when they came out of hiding. Indeed, when they did return, the three were murdered. Violence did not stop there, as James Asher's house was burned to the ground, leaving his widowed wife with three children to raise. After James Asher's demise, his son Charles, Hoffa's second cousin, was murdered by an acquaintance in 1888. His maternal side did not fare better, for his great-grandfather, Stephen Riddle Jr.'s home was the scene of the first murder in Green County, Indiana, in 1883. When Jimmy Hoffa was born in 1913, America was rapidly changing. It was the beginning of a new industrial revolution with mass manufacturing and new inventions to ease day-to-day living. Few had electricity but it was just a matter of time before parlor rooms lit up across the country. Motor vehicles started to appear on American streets, and the horse and buggy traffic slowly came to an end. Massive numbers of immigrants, mainly from Europe, started to swell American cities For most people, hard labor was the only way to support a family. John Cleveland Hoffa was no exception. Jimmy's father labored in a Pennsylvania coal mine under deplorable conditions. In 1920, John Hoffa died of black lung disease. Seven-year-old Jimmy was old enough to understand his

father was literally "worked to death" and he would remember that for the rest of his life. Hoffa's mother kept
the family together by doing laundry for well-to-do families in town while Jimmy and his brother Billy shined
shoes and delivered the clothes their mother washed to
make extra money.

Hoffa's daughter, Barbara Ann (Hoffa) Crancer, a St.
Louis County (Missouri) associate circuit court judge, recalled, "Dad told me a story one time about some bullies
that roughed the boys up and caused the laundry to be
dumped out of the basket and get dirty and their mother
would have to wash it again . . . Well, they took care of
these boys in good order." Brazil, Indiana, town biographer, Ms. Jessie Thomas said, "Jimmy was always self-
conscious about how he looked . . . being short gave him
a complex and he had to fight a little harder and show
more muscle." By 1922, Jimmy's mother was finding it
difficult to support her young family. A coal strike in
Pennsylvania made things worse and Viola decided to
move her family to Clinton, Indiana. The small town of
several hundred was not much better, and in 1924, Viola
Hoffa packed up her family and moved to Detroit. Arriving in the thriving city of almost one million, Viola found
a modest apartment on Merritt Street on the city's brawl-
ing working-class west side. Viola managed to get a job in
an auto parts factory, polishing radiator caps and working
in a laundry on the side. Jimmy found it difficult to adjust
to urban life with the neighborhood kids. They taunted
him, calling him a hillbilly. It took a few weeks for him to
show the local street toughs he wasn't going to put up
with the name-calling. Small in stature but tough as a

catcher's mitt, he stood his ground, winning respect and acceptance with his fists. Even with two jobs, Jimmy's mother still couldn't make ends meet. To help out, twelve-year-old Jimmy found a weekend job near his home at the Kroger Grocery and Baking Company bagging potatoes. As described in *Biography – Jimmy Hoffa* on The History Channel, a friend of Hoffa's, Walter Murphy, urged him to get into the food business. "No matter what happens, people have to eat," he said. "The family needed money and they didn't need him in school, so he sacrificed his education and had to go to work . . . he got a job where he could make small amounts of money," his son, James Hoffa Jr., recalled. At the end of the Roaring Twenties, Americans found themselves in the grips of the Great Depression. The City of Detroit was hit hard. Industries laid off thousands of workers and bread lines formed across the city.

Frank Murphy, the mayor, led the country in supporting state and federal welfare programs to help people through the economic crisis. It took five long years before Detroit began to get out of its economic quagmire and show its industrial strength through the resurgence of the automobile industry. Detroit was back. At the end of the 1930s, Detroit and the Teamsters were ready to take their place on the national stage.

After the attack on Pearl Harbor on December 7, 1941, the United States shifted its industrial muscle from civilian use to the war effort. Nowhere was that more visible than in Detroit. With its gigantic manufacturing base and massive influx of new workers from the deep south, Detroit earned a new moniker—Motor City . . . the Arsenal of Democracy. Twenty-eight-year-old James R. Hoffa was ready to ride on its coattails. In March, 1936, a group of female laundry workers approached Hoffa for advice in organizing a strike. He could not help noticing one of the women, a 17-year-old Polish beauty named Josephine Poszywak. He later wrote about the moment, *I felt I had been hit on the chest with a blackjack.* A brief courtship followed and they were married that fall by a justice of the peace. However, not everyone was happy about the marriage, especially Jimmy's mother. Hoffa's daughter, Barbara Ann Crancer, recalls her grandmother as a stern person. "My memories of her were scary. She didn't approve of the marriage of my mother and father and I'd say my mother's family didn't approve either. They thought of him as a hillbilly and the other side thought of her as a Pollack," she said. Nonetheless, their families' disapproval only made their relationship stronger and closer. "My parents were kind of opposites . . . my dad did not drink or smoke his whole life. My mother liked a good time . . . liked a cocktail and loved to have parties. My dad would call her the sergeant because she was the only one that could boss him around. She would tell him when he came home what different chores needed to be done and he always would cheerfully do them." Although family life for Hoffa was important, Jimmy was happiest on the job fighting battles for the Union. At the age of 24, he was elected president of Local 299, and under his strong leadership membership soared from 250 to 4,000. Most were truckers and warehouse workers and to them he was one the guys. There was no stopping Jimmy Hoffa now.

CHAPTER THREE

THE TEAMSTERS

James Riddle Hoffa's rise to power with the Teamsters was a long and brutal one. Looking back at the origins of the Teamsters provides a glimpse of Hoffa's ascent to president of the Teamsters Union. It all started in 1887 when the American Federation of Labor (AFL) assisted in forming local unions of Teamsters. Historic references to early freight transportation refer to "Teamsters" as those who drove teams of horses pulling huge wagons. The work was hard, giving the Teamsters a reputation of being "tough as nails" and street savvy.

Eleven years later in 1898, the AFL formed the Team Drivers' International Union (TDIU). In 1901, a group of Teamsters from Chicago split with the TDIU and formed the Teamster National Union. Under the leadership of Albert Young, the new 28,000-strong Union, which had 47 locals, advocated higher wages and shorter hours. Young applied for membership in the AFL and soon after, the AFL leadership asked the fledgling Union to merge with TDIU. In 1903, they joined forces to establish the International Brotherhood of Teamsters (IBT), which is now affiliated with the American Federation of Labor (AFL). In a raucous convention, Cornelius Shea was elected the first Union's president, but not without controversy. A rival by the name of John Sheridan, president of the Ice Drivers Union of Chicago, accused Shea of embezzlement and tried to prevent his election. But despite Sheridan's effort, Shea won by a vote of 605 to 480.

The Teamsters became vital to the labor movement (AFL), for they could paralyze the movement of goods through strikes. Commerce would stop dead in its tracks, which gave the Union extraordinary power. With the power came unscrupulous Teamster leaders who were able to demand bribes in order to avoid strikes. This opened the door for organized crime to jump in and demand a piece of the action.

It was not a secret that Cornelius Shea and the new Teamsters Union was corrupt. John R. Commons, labor historian, concluded that during Shea's time, the Teamsters were more a criminal organization than a legitimate Union. During the first three years of his tenure, a few major strikes occupied his time. The first one was the Chicago City Railway strike in November 1903, when Teamsters employed by the railway company went on strike. Shea tried to stop sympathy strikes by other Teamster locals but three locals walked out and later disaffiliated themselves over the sympathy strike issue. In 1904, a sympathy strike supporting 18,000 striking meat cutters in Chicago turned into riots before the massive use of strike breakers persuaded Shea to make his members go back to work. By 1905, Shea had expanded the Union numbers to almost 50,000 in 821 locals in over 300 cities, making it one of the biggest Unions in America. That same year, more than 10,000 Teamsters went on strike in support of locked-out tailors at Montgomery Ward. During the strike, it was revealed to newspapers that Shea was living in a whorehouse with a nineteen-year-old waitress and spending most of his time hosting parties. As a result, public support for the work stoppage collapsed. Yet, despite the bad press, Shea won re-election on August 12, 1905, by a vote of 129 to 121 and again in 1905 and 1906. Shea's appeal started to wane after his trial, stemming from the Montgomery Ward strike. Although the proceedings against him ended in a mistrial, his popularity plummeted. Shea promised to resign the presidency once the trial ended, but went back on his word. The move set the stage for the election of Daniel J. Tobin of Boston in August, 1907. Tobin faced opposition for three successive years (1908, 1909, and 1910) but never challenged after that. He remained president of the Teamsters until his retirement in 1952.

With Tobin at the Teamster helm, the Union began to expand rapidly. He urged the development of "joint councils" with which all local Unions had to affiliate, and it began serving as a breeding ground for up-and-coming leadership. Tobin encouraged agreements that covered all employers in any given industry, and this development

provided a cohesiveness amongst members not seen before. To bring discipline, he discouraged strikes and encouraged employers to sign contracts on the dotted line,
legitimizing the relationship between employer and em-
ployee. The 1930s became a time to stand up for workers'
rights and the rally-cry took the form of a song, "Solidarity Forever," written by Ralph Chaplin:

*It is we who plowed the prairies, built the cities where
they trade,*
*Dug the mines and built the workshops, endless miles
of railroad laid,*
*Now we stand outcast and starving mid the wonders
we have made.*
But the Union makes us strong!
Solidarity forever!
Solidarity forever!
Solidarity forever!
For the Union makes us strong!

By 1932 Teamster membership reached 82,000.
When the USA entered the Second World War in 1941,
paying membership in the Teamsters stood at an astonish-
ing 530,000 members, making the Union the fastest growing and most powerful labor organization in the United
States. As the Union increased in numbers, so did accusations of widespread corruption. Yet, despite the rumors,
Franklin Roosevelt, needing a base in the labor movement, appointed Tobin to be the official White House liai-
son to organized labor and to chair the Labor Division of
the Democratic National Committee. His influence ex-

panded when he was appointed the special representative to the United Kingdom and given the responsibility to investigate the labor movement there. Considered three times for Secretary of Labor, Tobin twice refused the prestigious post. While campaigning in the 1944 election, President Roosevelt gave his famous "Fala speech" in Washington, D.C., before the convention of the International Brotherhood of Teamsters, Chauffeurs, Warehousemen and Helpers of America. Addressing the Republican charges that he had left Fala, his Scottie, behind on the Aleutian Islands while on tour there and had sent a U.S. Navy destroyer at considerable cost to the taxpayers to retrieve him, Roosevelt demonstrated his showmanship to the fullest while further reinforcing the power base for the Union leader.

WILLIAM HRYB

CHAPTER FOUR

HOFFA'S EARLY UNION LIFE

Jimmy Hoffa left school at fourteen in 1927, lying about his age to get a job bagging groceries at Kroger Grocery Company after the stock market crash in 1929. Later, Hoffa took a job unloading produce trucks for 32 cents an hour. Two-thirds of his wages were redeemable for food. Considering the growing unemployment and food lines, the arrangement was appealing to many of the workers who needed the peace of mind of putting food on the table for their families. The downside to the job was that warehouse workers were required to report at 4:30 p.m. for a 12-hour shift, but they only got paid for the time they actually unloaded produce. Unable to leave the premises while waiting for produce arrivals, the workers sat idle.

Retired Teamster Roland McMaster remembered the way things were run on The History Channel, *Biography – Jimmy Hoffa,* "All the workers at this time were a depressed group . . . they had no money, were broke, and really didn't have nothing," he said. Joe Konowe recalled, "The workers had no protection on the job, and with wages so low, they decided to organize themselves into a local Union." As the country fell into the grips of the Depression, most of the men at Kroger's were cautious. But not Hoffa. The policy of not getting paid while waiting for shipments did not sit well with Hoffa, and one night in May of 1931 he courageously called for a work stoppage as the men were unloading trucks filled with crates of strawberries. Bobby Holmes, a long-time friend said, "We unloaded half the truck and left it wide open, so it lost all its refrigeration . . . we refused to unload the rest of the truck and everyone got excited." Arthur Sloane, Hoffa's biographer, wrote, *The men were inspired by Hoffa and decided right then and there not to unload the strawberries until management signed a Union contract with them.* The following morning, Kroger officials decided to meet with the 18-year-old rabble-rouser, as long as he could persuade his fellow workers to resume their duties. After several days of hard negotiating, Hoffa succeeded in winning a contract, their first ever. Hoffa was ecstatic. He had found his calling. His son, James Jr., recalled, "Even at an early age, my father was obviously a very charismatic person. At seventeen years of age, he was out saying, "This is what we are going to do, or we're going to strike." After his success at Kroger's, local Union leaders were impressed with the young man, and a year later, nineteen- year-old Hoffa was offered a job as an organizer with Teamsters Council 43 in Detroit.

Hoffa's combative and quarrelsome nature soon came to the attention of Union militants like Farrell Dobbs, a radical Trotskyite who was becoming a rising star in the Teamsters. From Dobbs, Hoffa learned the lessons of organizing and bargaining. Even though he rejected Farrell Dobbs' politics, he took some of Dobbs' teachings as rules to follow. Hoffa learned to take allies wherever you could find them, even if it meant getting help from unsavory types like mobsters.

Hoffa was brutal, aggressive, tough and profane. His bullying tactics and penchant for being devious and sometimes unscrupulous became a trademark. Unforgiving with a passion, he was innately intelligent and had the uncanny ability to learn quickly and master what was absolutely necessary. He could be charming and witty as well, which helped him to be an effective organizer. Despite the pitfalls involved in going up against established companies that were used to having their own way, Jimmy Hoffa took to the rough and tumble of Union activities immediately. His determination to succeed, sometimes using force, was his calling card. In the early days, companies would hire mobsters to intimidate workers and break up strikers' picket lines. To counter company tactics, Hoffa forged his own relationship with gangsters. Frank Ragano, Hoffa's attorney recalled, "He came to the realization that he needed muscle and so he made a deal with the Mafia, and all he wanted them to do was stay out of the strikes and just sit on the sidelines without fighting." Arthur Sloane, Hoffa's biographer, said, "He developed alliances with mobsters in Cleveland, Chicago, New York and northern New Jersey believing he was just recognizing reality." Hoffa would use the Mob as an effective tool but it was a deal with the devil.

Teamster officials discovered they had a firebrand to advance their cause, and at the age of 22, Hoffa was appointed business agent of Teamsters Local 299 in Detroit. It was a debt-ridden, run down Union with only 250 members. Officials believed Hoffa could breathe new life into the group, and they soon found out he relished the challenge. Teamster Bob Holmes recalled, "In negotiations, Jimmy had a saying . . . he said to me, 'Bob, whenever we go into negotiations, don't get up and leave - let the bastards get tired and maybe we can whip 'em.'" Hoffa lived by the credo that Unions were workers whose basic purpose was to protect, promote and serve the rights of the worker, such as providing safe working conditions and decent wages. Recognizing that companies would do anything to restrict workers' rights to get higher wages for their work, Hoffa was adversarial. During the 1920s and 30s it was common for companies to exploit and abuse workers' rights in order to take advantage of profits. Consequently, Unions became more militant by organizing strikes. Companies initiated the practice of hiring strike breakers, sometimes using baseball bats and truncheons to stop a strike action. Because of the violence, Union discontent exploded across every region in the country. Organizers like Hoffa were determined to represent workers and make sure they weren't going to get pushed around.

The rapid growth of the Teamsters in the 1930s and 1940s gave regional Union leaders significant political power, and with that came power struggles. Union membership in 1949 reached one million; however, by this time long-time Teamster boss Daniel Tobin's support was deteriorating. His leadership after almost five decades in power was being challenged vigorously. Dave Beck, who was elected an International vice president in 1940, was becoming a serious threat to Tobin's power base. In 1946, Beck successfully overcame Tobin's opposition and won approval of an amendment to the Union's constitution that created the post of executive vice president. The following year, Beck won the election to fill the position, lining himself up as a contender for the leadership that Tobin had held since 1907. In 1948, allied with 35-year-old firebrand James R. Hoffa, Beck effectively seized control of the Union.

Four years later in 1952 and with fading support, President Daniel Tobin announced his retirement. Dave Beck was elected general president in 1952 and the new leader moved fast. Beck quickly pushed through a number of important changes intended to make it harder for a challenger to unseat a president or reject his policies. He was the first Teamster president to negotiate a nationwide master contract and a national grievance arbitration plan while establishing organization drives in the deep south and east. With his considerable power, Beck built the lavish Teamster headquarters known as the "Marble Palace" in Washington, D.C. His intervention in a construction and milk strike in New York City and refusal to intervene in a northeastern trucking strike created major political problems for him. Beck's soon-to-be rival, Jimmy Hoffa, perceived Beck to be ineffective and began to challenge him on various Union policies and decisions. There was no mistake, Hoffa was aiming at unseating Beck as president at the next Union election scheduled in 1957.

The 1950s were promising to be another decade of tremendous growth for the Teamsters, with Hoffa clearly focusing on becoming the boss. Dan Tobin had held the reins for 45 years but was steadily losing control because many in the rank and file were branding him weak and old. Dave Beck, the natural successor to Tobin as vice president, was the leader of the large and aggressive Western Conference of Teamsters who pioneered some major wage and benefit improvements for its members. Beck thought he would be a shoe-in for reelection in 1957, but growing discontent with his leadership was widening. His reputation as a fence-mender and being politically savvy were admirable traits, but Beck had a race on his hands. Rank-and-file members were starting to rally around Jimmy Hoffa, the young, brash, aggressive leader from Detroit who headed the Central States Conference. The marked differences between Hoffa and Beck were like day and night.

Members of the Union believed that a Teamster leader should not be too far from the picket line, and with Hoffa he was often out front. His reputation as a tough negotiator appealed to Union members, matching and in some cases outpacing Dave Beck's wins from employers. Hoffa's popularity was soaring. Always willing to hear grievances from the rank and file, Hoffa struck a chord with the membership, which enabled him to put himself in the running for the top job.

Some Union members thought Hoffa was taking pay-offs, but most of them believed he was using the money not for his benefit, but to accumulate power for the Union. The opposite was true for Beck. He began to distance himself from Union members by acting like a wealthy businessman. Money that came his way by payoffs and extortion did not go to benefit the Union, but went to line his own pockets. He lavishly awarded himself with expensive homes and trappings of the rich. To many Union members, this was the last straw; and as the Teamster convention approached in 1957, it was apparent Dave Beck's days as Union leader were numbered. At the 1957 convention, 44-year-old Hoffa was elected president of the International Brotherhood of Teamsters. He had fulfilled his life-long dream.

Although Hoffa was triumphant in winning the top job as Union leader, a gathering storm began to overshadow Hoffa's election. The McClellan Committee hearings on corruption in the Teamsters Union were gaining momentum. In an excerpt from his acceptance speech, Hoffa proclaimed his goals, principles, and concerns about the McClellan hearings: *Brothers, brother Teamsters, one and all. I want to express from the bottom of my heart my thanks for the action taken here today by the delegates in a free and democratic election in selecting me as the president of this International Union. I say to you that we face the serious situation of bitter anti-Union legislation unless the labor movement begins to fight for due process and an end to one-sided and unproved accusations. If we become too timid to fight for what is right and just, we will lose in the legislatures what we have won on the picket lines. As*

*has been said on many occasions by such leaders as John
L. Lewis, there is more than enough legislation on the local, state and federal books to handle and prevent whatever corruption there may be within the ranks of labor.
There has been a concentrated effort to bring disunity and
confusion upon us.*

*We cannot ignore the fact that certain outside pres-
sures want to dominate or destroy this Union. We Teamsters have not lost our unity, and we shall not lose it. I
have no fight with the McClellan Committee, nor have I
any desire to obstruct a true and honest investigation. Investigations by committees of Congress to aid in legislation have a useful and proper place in America. But when
a Congressional committee concentrates on a personal
attack or misuses its power, it can be dangerous for all of
us. Something is wrong when a man may be judged guilty
in the court of public opinion because some enemy or
some ambitious person accuses him of wrong-doing by
hearsay or inference. What is happening to our historic
principle that a man is innocent until proven guilty?
Something is wrong when newspaper headlines have more
force than the findings of a court of law, or a jury of one's
fellow-men. Something is wrong when some Americans
begin to find fault with the Bill of Rights for which our
people have bled and died. The law should not be a weap-
on of politics. We are taught that our law is the backbone
of our democracy. Let's not write law on the front pages
of newspapers. Let us keep law in the statute books and in
the courts of justice . . . Let no outsiders weaken us by de-
stroying that unity. Let no outsiders by propaganda weak-
en the confidence of our rank and file in their leadership.*

Let us bury our differences; let us work together as a team; let us stand united, let us serve the interests and protect the welfare of our membership every hour of every day. By closing ranks, by settling our differences peacefully and democratically within our own house, we can move forward to build a greater and stronger Teamsters International Union.

WILLIAM HRYB

CHAPTER FIVE

HOFFA'S CHAUFFEUR / MARVIN ELKIND

"I got a job as a busboy at the Copacabana, which was owned at the time by Lou Walters, Barbara Walter's father and in order to work at the Copacabana you had to be a member of the Teamsters," said Marvin Elkind in the book *The Weasel: A Double Life in the Mob* by Adrian Humphreys. In the early 1950s, the former prizefighter from Toronto, Canada, became Jimmy Hoffa's personal driver in New York City where the Teamsters had an office at the Loews Midtown hotel.

Nine-year-old Marvin landed in a foster home when Children's Aid officials branded him incorrigible. By age eleven, Marvin was sentenced to a five-year stint in reform school. His life began as a struggle. He had to be dragged out of his mother's womb with forceps in March 13, 1934. His family emigrated from Romania, settling in Cabbage Town, a rough immigrant neighborhood in Toronto where disputes were settled without the presence of the cops whenever possible. For a poor immigrant Jewish girl, his mother Beatrice was well educated for the times and completed high school. Her handwriting was judged so exquisite that it was exhibited at the Canadian National Exhibition. Her talent soon earned her a job at a shipping office where she met Aaron Elkind, seven years her senior. Born in 1904, Aaron Elkind, Marvin's father, came to Canada from Russia in 1927 with his younger brother Morris to join their brothers, Sam and Harry who had arrived earlier with their father, Menachem, a Hebrew teacher in nearby Hamilton.

Aaron and Beatrice were married in 1931 and three years later Marvin was born. "My father was a bad guy," Marvin says, "He hung around with bad guys and was always getting into some trouble. My mother didn't know that at the time she married him. When she found out the kind of person he was, it was too late—she was pregnant with me. In those days, abortion was completely unheard of in the Jewish faith and so was divorce if you had a child. She said that if she hadn't had me, she would have left him. "My mother and maternal grandmother always blamed me for the fact that she was with him for so long. The person who always gave her support was Morris, my father's brother." Being Jewish, Aaron shunned the trappings of his faith while Morris always wore a yarmulke, the skull-cap Orthodox Jews wear. While Aaron swept floors, Morris got a better job as a cutter in the garment district. One night in 1937, Aaron and two friends planned to rob a bank. Someone tipped off the police and one of the robbers was killed. Aaron got away but later turned in the other guy, making a deal with the police allowing him to return to Russia. Three-year-old Marvin and his mother never saw him again. Six months after the failed bank heist, Beatrice married Marvin's Uncle Morris. Elkind describes himself as a "problem child," and he often got in trouble at school. Nine-year-old Marvin was sent to live in a foster home and it was not long before he discovered the criminal lifestyle. His new home was with an Italian family with meager resources. The Pasquale family ran a successful bootlegging enterprise, which gave Marvin a look at the other side of the law. Encouraged by his older foster brothers, he soon joined them on grocery store robberies in Toronto's West End. Elkind recalled, "We would go, the three of us . . . they would break open a window in the back, a basement window . . . I was probably eleven years old, a small kid. They would push me through and I would come upstairs and open the door and let them in. There was no such thing as safety deposit boxes in those days. The money was always in the store. If they got $50 they would take most of it and give me five bucks, which in those days was like a million. I used to take the money in one dollar bills so it would look like a big roll." Marvin soon learned that he had to compensate for his size because boys his age would pick on him. "It was very convenient for Jewish kids to learn either how to fight or how to run fast. I had a cousin who could do neither. Because my father was a partner with his father in the store, I had to fight for him, too. This was when I was seven or eight.

31

After school, he would wait for me to go home with him and I would get into the fights for him. It used to be a bit of joke because he was twice my size." At the age of eleven, Marvin ended up with a five-year sentence at a reform school. By the time of his release, he was ready for the dark side of the law. He eventually followed his foster brothers to New York City landing a job on weekends as a busboy at the legendary Copacabana. The night club was often frequented by underworld types and famous people. Marvin got a job working at the Stillman's boxing gym doing maintenance during the week to make extra money. One night in 1952, eighteen-year-old Elkind's life would suddenly change. "These guys would come in the Copacabana . . . Tony Salerno and Frankie Carbo. They were very scary and they yelled at everybody and everybody was scared to serve them . . . but they were big tippers," Marvin recalled. Elkind was also pursuing a boxing career in New York City. A regular customer at the gym where he trained at was a guy named Isador, a refined looking man who always had a bit of money. So Marvin made sure he was his friend by letting him in free to watch the boxers spar. "I used to always take good care of him, and he would always throw me a few bucks which was why I liked him," said Marvin.

Isador worked as a maître d' at the Copacabana, a nightclub on East 60th Street, near Central Park. Performers like Sammy Davis Jr., Frank Sinatra, Harry Belafonte, Dean Martin and Jerry Lewis played the Copa room regularly. Seeing qualities in Marvin as a good busboy, polite and not afraid to hustle, Isador offered him a job. "You know, I can get you a job as a busboy at the Copa—

evening and weekend work," he said. "The salary isn't big but the tips are good." The eighteen-year-old Marvin did not hesitate and found himself working at the most glamorous nightclub in the country. Elkind became a natural for this type of job since he was already an expert at getting himself accepted and keeping people happy. "You didn't have to be a genius for this job. You just had to kiss everybody's ass, and I was very good at that," he said. "A lot of it had to do with a bit of weakness in character—I found it easy to kiss their ass.

"In order to work at the Copacabana, you had to be a member of the Teamsters. It was easy, so I joined up and a group of Mr. Hoffa's associates used to come in there quite often. The staff was scared to serve them because they were tough guys and they tried to act it. Yes, they did their shouting and yelling, but I knew they weren't going to do anything. Besides, they were big tippers." Some of Marvin's fellow busboys and waiters would warn him about a certain bunch of loud guys and urged him to avoid them. After observing them for a few minutes, he knew right away they would become his favorites. Mobsters like Anthony "Fat Tony" Salerno, who later became the acting boss of Genovese Mafia family, and notorious shady boxing promoter Frank "Blinky" Palermo, who rigged some of the most outrageous boxing matches of the time, would come in to the Copa. Famous names in boxing including Sony Liston were on Blnky's payroll. Gangsters like Anthony "Tony Pro" Provenzano, later to be linked with the Hoffa disappearance and a member of the Genovese crime family and the Teamsters Union in New Jersey, was a frequent visitor to the nightclub. Most high

rollers at the Copacabana would buy a bottle of liquor for everyone at the table to share rather than ordering individual drinks. Sometimes Marvin would swipe a bottle of Scotch that had been brought out from behind the bar meant for another table. If it was left unattended for even a moment, he would stuff it under his apron and bring it over, free, for the gangsters. "They loved that . . . to these guys the only thing better than a good bottle of Scotch was a stolen bottle of Scotch, even though they paid out in tips to me what it would have cost to buy it," Marvin said. It was the way they worked and Marvin knew it. After a few months at the Copa, more than a few regulars joked that Marvin and Fat Tony looked like father and son. They both had fat, round faces, heavy cheeks and a wide neck. The biggest difference beside their 23 years was that Marvin always smiled. Marvin loved the comparison. Taking his cue from the remark, he started smoking cigars, just like Fat Tony did. It got to the point where Marvin always had a cigar either stuck in his mouth or held conspicuously in his hand. One night in June 1952, Marvin spotted Fat Tony and Tony Pro entering the Copa. The pair walked past the uniformed doormen and was greeted by hostesses. As the men were led to a table, Marvin was already hustling over to greet and smile, fill their water glasses and do his thing. Later that evening, as Marvin moved past the table, Tony Pro called out to him. "Hey, little Jew boy, get over here."

"Yes, sir," Marvin said.

Tony Pro said, "Friday is your last day here. We already spoke to the owners." Marvin was surprised. He enjoyed his work and loved the money. He also thought he was doing a good job and could not figure out why he was being fired.

"What'd I do?" he asked in dismay.

"Nothing. As of Monday, you're Jimmy Hoffa's driver. You're already a Teamster, we're just moving you. You'll be making more money than you are here and you won't have to pick up people's dirty dishes."

"I don't wanna be Jimmy Hoffa's driver."

"Kid, nobody's asking you," Tony Pro snapped.

"Look, I'm Canadian," Marvin said.

"That's exactly the idea," Tony Pro said. "Hoffa's driver was drafted and you being a Canadian, we don't have to worry about that. So I'm making you his new driver."

"But I don't know anything about the city," Marvin protested.

"You don't have to know anything about the city. We'll take you out on the weekend and teach you everything you have to know. Saturday morning, someone will pick you up . . . be ready."

Hoffa's driver had been drafted into the army days earlier, and with Elkind being a Canadian, Hoffa's handlers figured they didn't have to worry about him. Marvin recalled, "They took me out to a store and bought me three blazers, navy blue, royal blue and beige . . . six pairs of socks, half a dozen sport shirts, a coat and some pants." Marvin was excited about the sudden promotion, and after it was explained to him how things worked with Hoffa, Marvin was not sure what to expect.

"Hoffa was only in New York during the week. On the weekend he would go back to his family in Detroit and on Monday morning I'd pick him up at La Guardia and take him back on Friday." Elkind recalled, "Mr. Hoffa was a tremendously intimidating man . . . this man had no fear at all, of nothing, showed very little emotion and had completely no sense of humor, and was totally dedicated to the people that belonged to his Union. When you drive these people around, you learn a lot, and I'll tell you why—they don't know you're there. You become a piece of the car, just like an extra gear shift or brake." Chatter was something Elkind was strictly forbidden to do, and his employers made it clear from the start how serious they were about enforcing the rules. On his first day as Hoffa's driver, Elkind received his own lesson in high stakes big Union protocol. "So, I pulled up the car and I said, 'Good morning, Mr. Hoffa.' He said, 'You're Marvin,' and I said, 'Yes, sir.' He tells me to start driving and pull over up there, and these two guys get in the car, and these are his bodyguards. They got in the car and Hoffa says to me, 'Marvin, I've got cardinal rules and rules. If you break one of the rules, nothing serious is going to happen to you. If you break one of the cardinal rules, you won't be around the next day . . . now turn around and look at the boys.' Both of them opened up their coats to show me they were carrying pieces. It was very scary. And he told me the cardinal rule is: 'What you hear in this car, stays in this car!'" Marvin Elkind would follow the rules with no questions asked from 1953 to 1956. Years later when asked about the disappearance of Jimmy Hoffa, Elkind's face flushes, his voice rises, "I didn't see it happen, but there is no question in my mind that Mr. Hoffa is in the cornerstone of the Renaissance Centre Hotel in Detroit," he reveals.

"My reason is this: Mr. Hoffa had just got out of prison and was trying to get back the leadership of the Teamsters. In 1975 they were building the Renaissance Centre in Detroit aimed at rejuvenating the Detroit downtown area. At the time Jimmy Hoffa vanished July 30, 1975, concrete was a couple of weeks before it was ready to be poured. Now, when you pour concrete you have to put wooden forms down before you pour. It's a tremendous-sized hotel. A day or two after Hoffa went missing, every Teamster carpenter in the state of Michigan who was working on a high-rise or was building something recreational was called off on whatever they were doing and were re-assigned to put footings down so that they could get that concrete in right away. All hell broke loose . . . It was a mad rush to put the concrete in as soon as possible. So that's what makes me certain he's in there. Mr. Hoffa is in the concrete of the cornerstone at the towering Renaissance Centre Hotel in Detroit Michigan. I never saw concrete poured so fast in my life! The director of the Federal Bureau of Investigation was interviewed on television by Larry King and was asked where he thought Hoffa was. He said, 'I'm not sure but I think the Canadian driver is probably right.' Now, after this happened, there was a big meeting held across the Renaissance Centre called the Omni. At the meeting were the heads of the Detroit mafia led by Tony Giacalone. The session ended after three days, and for a change in scenery, Giacalone suggested they have something to eat. He said, 'Let's all go over to the Renaissance Centre . . . we'll have some breakfast there.' As we walked through the glassed walkway and crossed the dividing line between the Omni to the Renaissance, Mr. Giacalone says, 'Say good morning to Mr. Hoffa, boys!' which to me was proof enough that Hoffa's remains were in there.

"Mr. Hoffa was a fearless man, who wanted to do well for the rank-and-file Teamsters, there was no doubt about that. I don't think he was really a mobster or gangster . . . he was tough, but was not the way the world knew him. There was no question that he brought the Mafia in . . . he needed the muscle on the picket lines and he made a deal with them. I remembered one story that threw me a bit . . . a Hoffa associate by the name of Don Vito, a nice quiet grandfatherly or favorite uncle type of guy, was in the car with Hoffa one day. Sometimes when you were driving, Hoffa would yell at me because I made a bad turn. 'No big deal,' Don Vito would say, 'Jimmy, what are you yelling at the boy for? He's doing a good job.'"

CHAPTER SIX

HOFFA'S MAFIA LINKS

"**O**rganized labor will not sit idly by out of fear of a subpoena." The words rang out loud and clear as Jimmy Hoffa proclaimed his brand of leadership to almost 1.5 million Teamsters. Undaunted by Robert F. Kennedy's relentless pursuit in uprooting the criminal element from organized labor, Hoffa believed he was untouchable. What was there about Hoffa that made him think he was invincible? He was pugnacious, unrelenting, bombastic, highly ambitious and fearless. He was also careless, which eventually did him in.

"Remember our jurisdiction," said Tom Burke. Teamster organizer Joseph Franco turned to Burke and asked, "What's our jurisdiction?" Burke exclaimed, "The Teamsters' jurisdiction is anything that's got wheels. You got a wristwatch on? That's our jurisdiction. As long as it's got wheels on it, it belongs to us. Don't let any other fucking Union bother with it. Trucks, cabs, whatever. As long as it's got wheels." That would be the initiation to Union life in the mid-1940s for Joseph "Joe-Joe" Franco. Franco met Jimmy Hoffa in 1946 when he was a cab driver in Detroit and struck up a friendship that would last as long as Hoffa was alive.

When Jimmy Hoffa got involved in union politics during the mid-1930s, it was clear that the Mafia used him to advance their criminal activities. Yes, the Mafia used Hoffa and Hoffa used the Mafia. They made a good pair. In the early 1940s Hoffa's Detroit turf was targeted by a rival Union called the "Congress of Industrial Organizations" (CIO) which sent organizers to the Motor City in an attempt to unionize workers. Hoffa needed muscle to counter the intrusion and went to two Mafia guys named Sam Cook Perone and Frank Cappola. It did not take long for them to do their dirty work, and ran the CIO Union intruders out of town.

Historians have debated the fact that from Hoffa's acceptance of mobster help, as described in the book *The Rise and Fall of Jimmy Hoffa as Witnessed by his Strongest Arm* by J. Franco and R. Hammer, Hoffa went from a potential great labor leader to nothing more than a labor racketeer. Jimmy Hoffa never tried to hide or deny his relationship with the Mob. "These organized crime figures are the people you should know if you're going to avoid having anyone interfere with your strike, and that's what we know them for. . . We make it our business, and the head of any Union who didn't, would be a fool. Know your potential enemies and know how to neutralize them," Hoffa said.

Hoffa realized early in his career he needed the Mob to achieve what he wanted. It was crystal clear to Hoffa he had to work both sides of the street even though it meant breaking the law. The Mob needed Hoffa and Hoffa needed the Mob. You could barely distinguish them, one newspaper printed back in the 40s. *If it moves, sign it up* read the sign in Jimmy Hoffa's Union hall. Union organizing in the 1930's was dangerous and demanding. Organizers were getting a reputation that they were anarchists, rebels, and communists. The country was in a serious economic depression and people were desperate for jobs. Hoffa's frequent visits to Detroit's waterfront loading docks, warehouses and trucking companies made him a working class hero. He would come in with the bravado of a "street huckster." Hoffa recruited workers in retail stores, packing houses and breweries where he often ending up in street fights with hired thugs. "They were out to get us," Hoffa recalled. Receiving a small percentage of dues for each new member he recruited, Hoffa became an effective organizer for the Teamsters. Hoffa wrote years later: *Our cars were bombed . . . three different times someone broke into the office and destroyed our furniture. Cars would crowd us off the streets. Then it got worse . . . your life was in your hands every day. There was only one way to survive . . . fight back. And we used to slug it out on the streets. They found out we didn't scare and the police were no help. They would beat your brains in for even talking Union. The cops harassed us every day. If you* *went on strike, you got your head broken. The whole thing didn`t take months—it took years.*

Joe Franco said, "To this day, I still have the habit he (Hoffa) drilled into me about getting into a car. I put my right leg in and my left leg stays out, and then I start my car. If the car is rigged and you start your car that way, you have a 50-50 chance of surviving because if it blows up, it will blow you out of the car." In Hoffa's first year as the business agent for Local 299, police or strike breakers beat him up 24 times. "I was hit so many times with night sticks, clubs and brass knuckles that I can`t even remember where the bruises were," Hoffa said. The Union boss remembered being arrested 18 times in one 24-hour period on picket duty. "Every time I showed up on the picket line, I got thrown in jail. Every time they released me, I went back to the picket line." Hoffa spent one-third of his time in the office and stayed in touch with his people attending mass demonstrations where he showed up on the picket lines and signed up new members. "You got a problem, call me. Just pick up the phone," Hoffa said. He was quick to learn that spreading the Teamster message was best served by organizing long-haul truckers who traveled the country. He often would go up and down the highways, waking sleeping truck drivers and giving his Union pitch. During the lean years of the 1930`s, truckers knew they were easy targets for bandits and thieves as they slept in their trucks. Most held a heavy wrench or a three-foot tire iron while they caught a couple of winks before they resumed their long trips. Hoffa started his day at 8 a.m. and continued through the morning hours of the following day. He did not hesitate to use his own strong-arm tactics and was not shy to use them on rival Unions, notably the CIO. With his rapid-fire greeting, "Hi, I`m Jimmy Hoffa, organizer for the Teamsters, and I wonder if I could talk to you briefly?" Often he found employer-hired thugs planted in the trucks wanting to send him a strong message that the Teamsters were not wanted in their ranks. Hoffa made contacts with anybody who would listen. One of those guys was Moe Dalitz. Moe Dalitz controlled the laundries in Cleveland and was a major bootlegger during prohibition. Dalitz would go on to invest millions of dollars in Las Vegas and Southern California where he built the famous resort called "La Costa." Mobsters like Dalitz came up with ideas that led to creating pension and welfare funds. Teamster pension funds would become a cash cow. Morris "Moe" Dalitz became a racketeer and bootlegger who was mentioned in the same breath as Meyer Lansky and Benjamin "Bugsy" Siegel. Born in Boston in 1899, Dalitz`s father, Barney, operated a laundry and taught Moe the business as he was growing up. At a young age the family moved to Michigan where Barney operated a laundry in Ann Arbor, catering to university students. Moe Dalitz went on to open a string of his own laundries. Through his laundry business, Dalitz developed a close relationship with Jimmy Hoffa. They crossed paths in 1949 when the Detroit Teamsters Local demanded a five-day work week for laundry drivers. Laundry owners, including Dalitz, strongly opposed the Union`s position, and negotiations reached a brick wall with each side not budging. Being a shrewd businessman, Dalitz had the owner representatives bypass the local negotiator, Issac Litwak, and reached out to Jimmy Hoffa. Agents of the laundry owners asked what it would take for Hoffa to intervene on behalf of the owners. One of Hoffa's officials answered that $25,000 would do the trick. The owners agreed not to inform Litwak of the outcome. At a subsequent bargaining session, Litwak was confident he had the owners on the ropes. Late in the meeting, the door opened and in walked Jimmy Hoffa telling the group, "There'll be no fucking strike here . . . sign the contract with no five-day work-week." Stunned by the bravado and drowned out by support of the rank and file, Litwak had no choice but to comply. The transaction was no particular "big deal," but it did open the door for much bigger things ten years later when multi-million-dollar loans from the Teamster Pension Fund financed the Mob-controlled casinos in Las Vegas and sparked the growth of "Sin City." As the years passed, Moe Dalitz continued to use his friendship with Jimmy Hoffa to help facilitate loans required by the Las Vegas businesses. Through his association with Hoffa, Dalitz had a quiet but formidable influence on loans from the Teamster Central States Pension Fund. According to law enforcement investigators, one word from Dalitz could secure millions of dollars in low-interest financing. By 1966, the Aladdin and Caesars Palace casino resorts joined the growing list of enterprises dotting the popular Vegas strip. The famous Circus Circus Hotel and Casino followed two years later, and one could say the Teamsters were effectively involved with the gambling business. While Hoffa was serving time in a Lewisburg prison, Dalitz kept a low profile, remaining wisely out of the lime-light. At the end of the 1960's Las Vegas was the Mob's cash cow taking in millions of dollars in gambling money, thanks to Jimmy Hoffa and the Teamster Pension Fund. Prominent mobsters, such as Frank Coppola and Santo Perrone who operated in the Detroit area soon came to the attention of Hoffa. Frank Coppola was born in Sicily in 1899 and arrived in Detroit in 1922 eager to make a name for himself. The Sicilian immigrant rapidly established himself as a tough member of Detroit's underworld. An inveterate womanizer, Frank "Fingers" Coppola struck up a relationship with an attractive young member of the Teamsters Union clerical staff by the name of Sylvia Pagano. Pagano already knew several Detroit mobsters through her deceased husband, Sam Scaradino. The sexy-looking Pagano introduced Hoffa to Coppola, who arranged an introduction with Santo Perrone, Angelo Meli, and other highly placed members of Detroit's underworld. Hoffa needed the Mob's muscle and with the alliance, Hoffa soon was able to establish the Teamsters as a powerful labor union. However, there was a price to pay for the relationship. Trucking Unions in that era were heavily influenced and in many cases controlled by elements of organized crime. For Hoffa to unify and expand trucking Union groups, there was no question; he had to make accommodations and arrangements with gangsters in the Detroit area.

CHAPTER SEVEN

HOFFA AND THE ROBERT KENNEDY FEUD

S tarting in 1953and again in 1954, investigating committees from the House of Representatives were probing evidence of corruption within the Teamsters Union. Originally chaired by Representative Clare Hoffman, he was replaced by Wint Smith, a Republican from Kansas. Smith had his sights on Hoffa. Not missing a beat, Hoffa employed former Republican Governor Payne Ratner from Kansas as his attorney, and soon after, the investigations stopped. Reports of political pressure applied by Ratner, like a well-placed tourniquet, took the heat off the Teamsters for the time being. Jimmy Hoffa proved that he could pull the strings from the shadows.

Hoffa gained considerable support during the early 50s, which put him on track to contest Dave Beck's leadership of the Teamsters. Beck was one of the most powerful and outspoken labor leaders in America and the first of a series of Teamster presidents to go to jail. Serving as the president of the International Brotherhood of Teamsters from 1952 to 1957, Beck invoked the Fifth Amendment against self-incrimination 117 times during the McClellan Committee hearings on corruption in the labor union movement. He was found guilty and convicted two years later of federal income-tax evasion and state embezzlement charges for stealing $1,900 from the sale of a Union-owned Cadillac. He served 30 months in prison before being paroled in 1964. After Dave Beck was forced out, newly elected president Jimmy Hoffa became the prime target. The McClellan Committee uncovered wide-spread evidence, alleging management, the underworld, public officials and labor leaders worked to intimidate and cheat rank-and-file Union members. Charging ahead, a brash, young Robert Kennedy zeroed in on how Unions were bought and sold. The relatively new medium of television brought the sensational hearings to a wide national audience estimated at over 1.2 million, giving the American public a first glimpse of what had been long suspected. The *Chicago American* newspaper's strong criticism of Robert Kennedy for his overbearing zealous behavior during the hearings worried his father, Joseph P. Kennedy Sr. Concerned about Robert Kennedy's conduct, he rushed to Washington D.C. to see for himself if his son was endangering John Kennedy's political future. JFK had his sights set on running in 1960 for the presidency, and there was reason to believe that Robert Kennedy could derail his brother's chances. Joseph Kennedy's close connections to the Mob fueled the intrigue of the extraordinary hearings. It was long rumored that Joe Kennedy made his fortune with the help of organized crime. During prohibition, Joseph Kennedy and well known Mafia figure Frank Costello partnered in selling illegal liquor to a thirsty public. Running booze became an enormous money maker, especially when Joe Kennedy became the sole dealer for all of the Scotch whiskey coming out of Scotland. Kennedy was often seen playing golf with Mafia kingpins like Johnny Roselli and Sam Giancana in Lake Tahoe, fueling gossip about his Mob connections. When Jimmy Hoffa was ordered to appear before the McClellan Committee hearings, Robert Kennedy showed no mercy. He was determined to put the cocky labor leader in his place. The national audience observed an unmistakable hatred of one another. Like prize fighters, they went toe-to-toe with neither one backing off. For the pugnacious labor boss, the idea that Kennedy would get the best of him turned his stomach. "To hear Kennedy when he was grandstanding in front of the McClellan Committee, you might have thought I was making as much out of the pension fund as the Kennedys made out of selling whiskey," Hoffa scoffed. It was obviously a reference to Robert Kennedy's father, Joseph, who made millions from prohibition. "Hell, I'm not saying I'm an angel, but when it came to dirty tricks, I couldn't hold a candle to the Irish Mafia." Robert Kennedy and Jimmy Hoffa first met at a private dinner party on February 19, 1957. A mutual acquaintance, Eddie Cheyfitz, who was Hoffa's lawyer, thought it would be a good idea for both men to get to know each other before the McClellan Committee hearings got underway. In his book titled *The Enemy Within*, Kennedy describes the encounter: *Both Cheyfitz and Hoffa met me at the door—Hoffa with a strong, firm handshake. Immediately, I was struck by how short he is–only five feet and a half. We walked into the living room of Cheyfitz's elaborately decorated house, but chatted only a few minutes before going in to dinner. The three of us were alone. Hoffa, I was to discover, can be personable, polite and friendly, but that evening he maintained one steady theme in his conversation throughout dinner and for the rest of the evening. "I do to others what they do to me, only worse," he said. "Maybe I should have worn my bulletproof vest," I suggested. From that first meeting, it seemed to me that he wanted to impress upon me that Jimmy Hoffa is a tough and rugged man.* Kennedy wrote of Hoffa's behavior that evening, *When a grown man sat for an evening and talked continuously about his toughness, I could only conclude that he was a bully, hiding behind a façade.* Hoffa found Kennedy condescending and a "damn spoiled jerk." He also had the impression that Kennedy "puzzled over the fact that a kid from a poor family, lacking education, could rise to the top of the largest Union." It was crystal clear from the dinner meeting that Kennedy and Hoffa would not get along. Kennedy recalled, *As I was going out the door, Hoffa said, "Tell your wife I'm not bad as everyone thinks I am." I laughed. Jimmy Hoffa had a sense of humor. He must have laughed at himself as he said it. In view of all that I already knew, I felt that he was worse than anybody aid he was.* In the next two and half years, Hoffa and Kennedy would battle it out and, in the process, set a course of unpredictable consequences. The McClellan Committee hearings exposed a lot about the two adversaries. A famous exchange that the public witnessed on television offers a glimpse of the contempt they held for one another. "You have people in Detroit—at least fifteen—who have police records. You have Joey Glimko in Chicago. I say you're not tough enough to get rid of these people," said Kennedy.

"Well, I don't propose . . ." replied Hoffa.

"You haven't moved against any of them!" Kennedy interrupted.

"I don't propose to act tough and I will follow the constitution of the International Union. I don't get frightened too easily. I don't intend to leave the impression that has been stated publicly that I am controlled by gangsters. I am not controlled by them."

"While leaving the hearings after these people testified, did you say, 'That S.O.B.—I'll break his back?'" asked Kennedy.

"Who?"

"You!"

"I said that to who?"

"To anyone! Did you make that statement after those people testified before the committee?"

"I never talked to any of them."

"I'm not talking about THEM. Did you make that statement here, in the hearing room after the testimony was finished?" said Kennedy.

"Not that I know of . . ."

"Well, who did you make the statement about? Whose back were you going break, Mr. Hoffa?"

"I don't remember!"

"Who's back were you going to break, Mr. Hoffa?"

"A figure of speech . . . I don't know who I was talking about, and I don't know what you're talking about!" said Hoffa.

The exchange was visceral. Television audiences got their fill of drama and true animosity the two adversaries shared. John F. Kennedy, who was a member of the McClellan Committee said, "I'm not satisfied when I see men like Jimmy Hoffa in charge of the largest Union in the United States still free!" Hoffa countered, "There are those that will tell you that 'Hoffa is a rackets man. Hoffa is part of the underworld . . . he tried to arouse a revolution with this International Union . . . first with the hearings with the McClellan Committee and *little* Bobby Kennedy.'" The name calling and accusations continued unabated.

"Mr. Hoffa, would you allow as a Teamster official a man who is a communist?" asked Kennedy.

"We don't have any communists in our Teamsters," replied Hoffa.

"Just answer the question!"

"Just a moment please. We don't have any communists that I know of." A few years after the hearings concluded, Hoffa was asked to give an opinion about his rival and nemesis, Robert Kennedy. "He wasn't a good attorney general and in all probability a worse senator— I'd hate to think what would happen if he became the President of the United States . . . we would probably have a fascist government." Hoffa and the American people would never find out. Kennedy was assassinated in June 1968, after winning the California primary and gaining an overwhelming lead as the Democratic candidate for the presidency of the United States. The McClellan hearings made Jimmy Hoffa famous. He was as well known as Elvis Presley in the late 1950s and the Beatles in the 1960s. Every newspaper in the United States was following the "Hoffa Hearings" as it was commonly called by media. Robert Kennedy appeared on the Jack Paar show on March 13, 1964. It was his first public appearance after his brother JFK was gunned down in Dallas, Texas, four months earlier. When Paar asked Kennedy to compare the faults of Dave Beck and Hoffa, he said, "Oh, there is no comparison between them, Hoffa and Mr. Beck," Kennedy said. "Mr. Beck was just a thief. Mr. Hoffa is a far more serious threat than Mr. Beck. What made Hoffa much worse was his willingness to build up the Union's power, to use it, and to defy the government. The Teamsters Union, as it is operated now by Mr. Hoffa, because of its control of transportation, is probably the most powerful institution in the United States next to the government." When Robert Kennedy became the attorney general, he recruited Walter J. Sheridan as a special assistant to investigate federal crimes involving the Teamsters. Sheridan had worked closely with Robert and John Kennedy during the McClellan hearings and later became regional coordinator for John F. Kennedy's 1960 presidential campaign. Under Walter Sheridan's control, the "Get Hoffa Squad's" full-time job was to bust Hoffa. Sheridan and his squad received their biggest break when Edward

Grady Partin decided after decades of dirty work for the Teamsters Union that he would work as an informant for the Kennedy administration. In jail at the time awaiting trial for embezzlement of Union funds and kidnapping, Partin was a close associate of Hoffa's; and to save his own skin, decided to cooperate with the government. Hoffa was blindsided when Partin testified against him. This led to a conviction of jury tampering and an eight-year prison term. Coming to Hoffa's defense, Supreme Court Justice Earl Warren later called the conviction an "affront to the quality and fairness of federal law enforcement." Hoffa went on trial in Chattanooga, Tennessee, in January 1964 on charges of tampering with the jury in the Test Fleet case two years earlier. The Test Fleet trial ended with a hung jury; however, Hoffa and various others were convicted of bribing members of the jury during the trial. The Court of Appeals affirmed the convictions. Edward Partin testified to various statements made to him by Hoffa. During the Test Fleet trial, Hoffa occupied a three-room suite in a hotel in Nashville where Partin often visited. Being on the inside, Partin provided federal agents proof that Hoffa was attempting to bribe members of the Test jury. The trial was over in four weeks with Hoffa being convicted. After the trial, Partin's wife received money from the government and all charges against Partin were dropped.

Hoffa faced another trial for the Sun Valley case which was a conspiracy to defraud the Teamster Pension Fund. Again, the jury brought in a guilty verdict and the once invincible Hoffa faced another five years in prison to run concurrent with the eight years he had already received. Hoffa was in serious trouble; however, he was not convicted of violating the Landrum-Griffin Act. The law was enacted in 1959 after the McClellan hearings as a response to the widespread publicity about corruption in certain American labor unions. The new law provided for penalties for labor officials who misused Union funds, who had been found guilty of specific crimes, or who had violently prevented Union members from exercising their legal rights.

If Hoffa had been convicted, he would have been banned from Union activities for the rest of his life. Having exhausted his appeals, Hoffa was ordered to report to Lewisburg Federal Prison in 1967 to begin his 13-year jail term.

The American public were getting familiar with Hoffa's notoriety. As the hearings drew to an end, criticisms of the Select Committee and Robert Kennedy were less frequent. Even though some lawmakers believed Kennedy's aggressive attacks on the moral issues of labor union activities endangered the constitution, Senator McClellan wanted to further investigate organized crime and its infiltration into the labor movement; but it had reached the limits of its jurisdiction and concluded no further investigations were to be made. In August of 1959, a second interim report denouncing Jimmy Hoffa and the Teamsters was released, and by the fall of 1959, it was apparent the Select Committee was not finding any more information that would justify continued hearings. Soon after Robert Kennedy resigned his position as the Select Committee's chief counsel on September 11, 1959, and took on the role

as his brother's campaign manager for his presidential bid
in 1960.

VANISHED

CHAPTER EIGHT

HOFFA AND MOB CONNECTIONS

James Riddle Hoffa's disappearance on July 30, 1975, remains a mystery—a cold case. An abundance of theories and speculation continues to captivate and intrigue a world audience. What happened to Jimmy Hoffa? Will we ever know? One thing for sure is, seven years to the day of his disappearance, Hoffa was declared legally dead in 1982.

Just weeks after Hoffa went missing, FBI agents compiled a list of nine strong potential suspects. The FBI knew Hoffa had gone to the Machus Red Fox Restaurant in Bloomfield Township in Michigan and was picked up in a certain car, supposedly to meet with Detroit mobsters Tony "Jack" Giacalone and New Jersey Mob kingpin "Tony Pro" Provenzano to iron out some differences. But that's where it ends. The case still haunts the FBI because it has never been solved. Even though the FBI believes Hoffa was "rubbed out" by the Mafia, the questions remain: who killed him and where are his remains if there are any? In the years that followed his disappearance, there have been numerous searches for Hoffa, all of them going nowhere. An extensive dig at a Michigan farm several years ago turned up nothing. Another dig in 2012, at a suburban Detroit home's drive-way, came with no results. Wild rumors where Hoffa's body might be still persist. Over the years, all kinds of gossip where Hoffa's remains were disposed of have come and gone with no evidence. Rumors that his body was entombed under Section 107 at the now-demolished Giants Stadium in New Jersey; hidden in the concrete foundation of Detroit's Renaissance Center; stashed under a horse barn; thrown into the Florida swamp; buried in a backyard swimming pool in Bloomfield Hills; weighted down in the Detroit River; crushed in a wrecking yard compactor; dissolved at a fat-rendering plant; buried in a gravel pit; and squeezed into a oil-drum and thrown into the toxic-waste dump in New Jersey made headlines but little else. Nobody has been arrested for the Union leader's likely murder, and his final seconds remain a mystery. With a thinning of those who were close to him, the enigma gets deeper and more mysterious. "Unfortunately, this has the markings of a great who-done-it novel without the final chapter," Prosecutor David Gorcyca was quoted as saying a few years ago. At the time, new DNA evidence, he said, was not enough to support state criminal charges in Hoffa's disappearance. The most recent disclosure (June 2013) had Jimmy Hoffa's body buried in a shallow grave about 20 miles from the Machus Red Fox Restaurant where he was last seen alive. In January of 2013, Tony Zerilli, a well-known Detroit mobster who was locked up in prison at the time of Hoffa's disappearance said in an interview to New York's NBC 4 News, "I'm as certain as I could possibly be. If I had money, I'd like to bet a big sum of money that he's buried there." He went on to declare, "I'd like to just prove to everybody that I'm not crazy." Zerilli has just come out with his self-published book titled *Hoffa Found* that was released earlier in the year but with no tangible evidence that his claim was true. Along with other famous vanished personages, the notorious labor leader's disappearance will be the source of rumors and speculation for years to come. Steven Brill, in his book titled *The Teamsters*, said, *The Mob had control of one of the nation's major financial institutions and one of the very largest private sources of real estate investment capital in the world.* Frank Fitzsimmons, Hoffa's successor, was a pushover for the Mob. Through Fitzsimmons, the Mob had access to a massive pension cache, favorable contracts and preferential handling. In later years, Mob control of the Union became strikingly evident when the FBI bugged a New York nightclub called the Parma Boys Social Club where they recorded Anthony "Fat Tony" Salerno discussing an upcoming Teamster presidential election of Roy Williams in June 1981. Frank Fitzsimmons had died of cancer in May of that year and Williams was favored to succeed Fitzsimmons. The evidence uncovered in the wire-tap ended up convicting Salerno in 1986 of rigging the election of Roy Williams. The Genovese crime family boss was later identified by federal prosecutors as a senior member of "The Commission," the ruling council of the five principal crime families in *La Cosa Nostra.*

Anthony "Fat Tony" Salerno, the cigar-chomping, gruff crime boss, ruled the deadly 200-member Genovese family, having influence over labor unions in Cleveland, the concrete industry in New York City, and considerable clout over the Miami waterfront. Howard Abadinsky, a professor of criminology at St. Xavier University in Chicago and author of several books on organized crime, said, "He was extremely powerful."Abadinsky compared Salerno to the reputed head of the Gambino family, Paul Castellano. "Castellano was perhaps first among equals, but Fat Tony would have been the other most powerful figure on the East Coast." Three years after the law caught up with the seventy-eight year-old gangster, he entered the prison system in 1989 with sentences of 100 and 70 years on separate federal racketeering convictions. The grim-reaper finally caught up with "Fat Tony" Salerno when he died of a stroke at the Medical Center for Federal Prisoners in Springfield, Missouri, in July 1992. Salerno was portrayed by actor Paul Sorvino in the gangster movie Kill the Irishman depicting "Fat Tony's" role in the gangland war between the Irish Mob boss Danny Green and the Cleveland Italian Mob led by Salerno.

Emerging from prison two days before Christmas in 1971, Jimmy Hoffa was a bitter man. Before going to prison in 1967 to serve a 13-year prison sentence, Hoffa had made it clear to Fitzsimmons that he still would be the boss and retain his title until he got out. Fitzsimmons was expected to follow orders. His major task was to get Hoffa out of jail and back into his office as president of the

Teamsters. His hand-picked caretaker successor, however, was beginning to get used to being the boss and was thinking about how he was going to keep the perks and power he now relished. Hoffa and Fitzsimmons had known each other since the 1930s when he joined the Teamsters as a dock worker in 1934. He later started driving a truck and became a business agent for a Detroit Teamster Local in 1937. Over the years, he was a loyal lieutenant of Hoffa's, but with Hoffa's legal troubles mounting, he began to distance himself from his longtime friend. Fitzsimmons became aware that it was an almost impossible task to have Hoffa freed with the Democrats in power. Colleagues of Robert Kennedy still controlled the Justice Department and were not going to be lenient on Hoffa's case. Meanwhile, Fitzsimmons' meager efforts to spring his boss from prison was greeted with disdain by government officials. The Democratic machine had no intention of releasing Hoffa and wanted him locked up as long as the law allowed. It soon became apparent to Fitzsimmons that Hoffa would remain in prison for a long time.

Sensing a change in government because of the disarray in the Democratic Party and failures in Vietnam, Lyndon Johnson announced his withdrawal from the presidential race on March 31, 1968. Frank Fitzsimmons set his sights on Richard Nixon and offered him Teamster support with money and votes. With the help of Fitzsimmons, Nixon won the 1968 election in a tight race. Fitzsimmons was finding that he liked Hoffa's job and enjoyed being the boss; and although he publicly called for the release of Hoffa from prison, the truth was he wanted to delay Hoffa's freedom until he figured out a way of dislodging him. Denied bail on three occasions, it became clear that the only way Hoffa would get an early release was to resign as president of the Teamsters. Even though he was stubborn and reluctant to relinquish the presidency, he agreed to let Fitzsimmons take over but with the agreement that he would get his position back after getting out. Little did Hoffa know Fitzsimmons had no intention in keeping his side of the bargain. A plan soon was hatched between Fitzsimmons and Nixon to pardon Hoffa, but with the provision he could not enter into any Union activities with the Teamsters until 1980. The only problem with that arrangement was that Hoffa knew nothing about it. When Hoffa learned of the stipulation after leaving prison he was livid and vowed to get the "small print" ruling overturned. As the 1972 election approached, Fitzsimmons threw his full Teamster support to Nixon's 1972 presidential campaign in which Nixon trounced McGovern in a lop-sided victory. The Machiavellian back-room deal gave Nixon and Fitzsimmons what they wanted, but it would lead to events of unforeseen consequences. When Frank Fitzsimmons took over as the leader of the Teamsters, he began to break up the power base Hoffa had built up over the last twenty-five years. Teamsters' leaders in regional and local areas of the country were the benefactors, gaining new power and influence. The new authority handed to the Union vice presidents was a veiled gift to the Mob. They knew they didn't have to go to one man as they did with Hoffa. All the gangsters had to do now was call a Teamster leader for a favor. Those who cooperated became rich. As soon after Fitzsimmons was elected president of the Teamsters after Hoffa's resignation, he declared to all his vice presidents, "I'm giving you the authority to run your own areas. If you get into trouble, don't come back to me. I don't want to hear about it. So don't get into trouble. In the meantime, you have full authority to run your areas and I hold you responsible for those areas." The new responsibilities were greeted with the question of how the vice presidents could get a little money out of this thing. The vice presidents could never talk to Hoffa that way, but Frank Fitzsimmons was an easy mark for his vice presidents. They persuaded him into making all of them general organizers at $40,000 a year on top of what they were already earning. All Fitzsimmons wanted to do was have a good time with all the trappings of being the Union boss. He didn't think twice about reaping the awards of his new position by increasing his yearly salary to $125,000, nearly twice what Hoffa made. There were three homes he could live in, too—one in California, one in Florida, and another in Washington. Fitzsimmons also had access to the $3.5 million jet that could fly him anywhere in the world, all expenses paid by the Union. He was getting used to the good life and didn't want to give up any perks of the job.

Unlike Hoffa, Fitzsimmons was able to devoid himself from the clamor of the press about Mob connections. The once trusted lieutenant was now able to concentrate on making new friends in the big labor movement and government circles. Fitzsimmons was beginning to think he didn't need Hoffa and was going to make sure that Hoffa wasn't going to take the position away. Robert

Kennedy was the chief counsel to the McClellan Committee before he resigned to run his brother's presidential bid. Rumors were beginning to swirl before the 1960 election that if Nixon lost, JFK was going to appoint his brother Robert attorney general in a new administration. The prospect scared Hoffa, leading to a half-a-million dollar contribution to Nixon's 1960 campaign funneled through Mafia kingpin, Carlos Marcello. The tactic also was all Hoffa needed to have land fraud proceedings dropped fueling suspicion that then Vice President Nixon was helping Hoffa. While Hoffa was in prison, he generously offered advice to his long time Teamster friend Joe Franco who was also doing time at Lewisburg. "Don't gamble, don't get too close to nobody, don't get involved, don't trust nobody because everybody's a stool pigeon— everybody, so nobody in here can tell on you if you don't open your mouth. When you take a shower, make sure you do it with the lights on and use your own soap because there are sick sons of bitches in here who take razor blades and break them in half and stick them in soap to cut you up. Don't take nothing unless you pay it right back."

Hoffa further advised his friend to "work hard, walk hard, exercise hard, play ball, do what you have to do, only do it hard. Because what will beat you is not the prison system but your own mind…. You've got to be able to get into that bunk and lay down and go to sleep." After all, Hoffa had been through it. He had learned that the routine he set for himself was what helped him to survive.

While Hoffa was serving time in Lewisburg, he met up with Carmine Galante, underboss of the Joseph Bonanno crime family. A dispute over the succession the crime family was happening at the time and made things more complicated than Bonanno cared for. The other New York crime families remained neutral during the so-called Banana Wars that took place between 1963 and 1969 but suddenly reversed when they learned two New York Mob bosses, Thomas Lucchese and Carlo Gambino, were being targeted for assassination. Accusing Bonanno's son, Salvatore Bonanno, of planning the plot, the syndicate's ruling council demanded the elder Bonanno to answer the charge. Not only did he refuse, he started raiding other Mob-controlled areas. The syndicate had enough. Joseph Bonanno was thrown out of the ruling council. Fearing for his life and possible federal charges Bonanno wisely went on the lamb from 1964 to 1966.

During that period, Bonanno managed to connect and develop a coalition with Mob bosses Carlos Marcello of Louisiana and Santo Trafficante of Florida. Since the heat was still on in New York, Bonanno shifted his operations to Arizona. The Mob troika rivaled the New York Mob in every way. As the president of the most powerful Union in the United States, Hoffa had a close working relationship with the New York crime families as well as a closer association with Mob bosses Marcello and Trafficante. Hoffa's prison pact with Galante made him an important person in the North-South Mob power rivalry. When Fidel Castro overthrew the Battista-controlled Cuba in 1959, years of Mob-controlled casinos and prostitution came abruptly to an end. Prior to the Cuban Revolution, the island was a playground to the rich and famous. Mobsters like Carlos Marcello and Carlos Trafficante who made millions off their operations in Havana were now forced to flee the island losing their gambling and heroin trade connections. Shortly after returning from a triumphant visit to the U.N. in 1960, Castro's cavalier attitude towards the United States was straining their relationship. The Cuban revolutionary was reaching out to the Soviets, much to the concern of the U.S. government. It didn't take long for Castro's star status to fade with the Kennedy administration. The Soviet-Cuban connection worried the administration so much that the CIA was called into action to remove the rebel leader. Gangsters like Santo Trafficante of Tampa, Florida, Carlos Marcello of New Orleans, Sam Giancana of Chicago, and mobster Russel Bufalino (Rosario Alberto Bufalino also known as McGee) of Pennsylvania were anxious to get their "turf" back and eagerly agreed to work with the intelligence agency in a direct action against Castro. A plot was hatched to get rid of Castro by any means possible, including assassination. Credible evidence points to a Jimmy Hoffa connection. The labor leader was purported to be a link in the plot as he was alleged to be the original middleman between the Mob and U.S Central Intelligent Agency. Hoffa had access to millions of dollars in Union pension funds and was later incriminated but never proven to have been funneling money for arms sales to both Battista and Castro factions. When the Bay of Pigs action fell apart, the Kennedy administration distanced itself from the Cuban exiles who attempted to overthrow Castro. A deep hatred aimed at President John Kennedy was the result as they felt betrayed. Just four months after JFK's inauguration on April 17, 1961, about 1,300 Cuban exiles armed with U.S. weapons landed at the Bahia de Cochinos (Bay of Pigs) on the southern coast of Cuba. Expecting to find support from the local population, the small army intended to march across the island to Havana. Soon after landing, it was apparent that support was not there and the exiles would lose. President Kennedy had the option of helping with U.S. air strikes against the defending Cubans but decided against it. Two days later on April 19, ninety exiles lay dead and the rest were taken prisoner. Kennedy's inaction precipitated a deep resentment within the American Cuban community as well as seriously embarrassing his fledgling administration. Many of the captured exiles were later ransomed by Cuban groups in the United States, sparking a decade's long struggle to rid Cuba of Castro. The new Cuban leader had no illusions and was convinced the Americans would attempt to take over the island again. The CIA's efforts to infiltrate Cuba can be traced to President Dwight Eisenhower when they started to train anti-revolutionary Cuban exiles for a possible invasion right after Castro forced Battista from the island. Because of the increasing tension with the leftist leaning Castro, Eisenhower broke off diplomatic relations in early January 1961 just before handing the presidential reins to John Kennedy. The dye was cast.

PHOTOS

Hoffa and Frank Fitzsimmons   Hoffa and Frank Sheeran

Teamsters Local 299 in Detroit   Hoffa and
                                  "Tony Pro" Provenzano

PHOTOS
(CONTINUED)

Fitzsimmons and Nixon

Hoffa at home - summer of 1975

Hoffa on *Life* cover   Hoffa election poster -1957

VANISHED

WILLIAM HRYB

CHAPTER NINE

HOFFA AND THE GOVERNMENT

Rumors that Hoffa, Marcello, and Trafficante had discussions about murdering President Kennedy surfaced, but no firm evidence supported the accusation. The innuendo that the three were in contact with the Dallas nightclub owner Jack Ruby who shot and killed Lee Harvey Oswald was startling. Members of the Warren Commission investigating the Kennedy assassination had some knowledge of the connection but curiously decided not to go further with it. A year before Hoffa disappeared, the U.S. Senate held closed-door hearings on the Mob's involvement in both the plot to assassinate Fidel Castro by poison and the Mob's involvement in the Bay of Pigs invasion. Chairing the Senate Select Committee was Senator Frank Church of Idaho. The committee heard testimony and collected evidence about the Mob ties to the April

1961 Bay of Pigs invasion and to a suspected Mob-CIA scheme to murder Fidel Castro. At the very beginning of the 1975 hearings, the CIA revealed to the Church Committee the Mob's involvement and assistance in the Bay of Pigs invasion and the existence of the CIA-Mob plot to kill Castro, called "Operation Mongoose." A few days before notorious mobster Sam "Momo" Giancana was scheduled to testify before the Church Committee, he was gunned down. With Giancana dead, the committee summoned Giancana's lieutenant, Johnny Roselli, to testify under oath behind closed doors. A few months later Roselli met the same fate as his former boss when police discovered his body stuffed in an oil drum. During the hearings, *Time* magazine's June 9, 1975, issue reported that Russell Bufalino and Sam Giancana were the crime bosses behind the Mob's ties to the CIA, the botched Bay of Pigs invasion, and the plan to poison Fidel Castro. Armed with volumes of testimony and the CIA's confession, the Church Committee ended up drafting legislation limiting the CIA's involvement in the affairs of independent countries. The legislation passed but became a hot topic again following the 9/11 tragedy involving a series of four attacks by the Islamic terrorist group al-Qaeda upon the United States in New York City and the Washington, DC metropolitan area. Some legislators believed the Church Committee had gone too far in curtailing the CIA's covert activities.

In the late 1950s the McClellan Committee had one objective: To uncover corruption in the labor movement and to put Jimmy Hoffa behind bars. Under Robert Kennedy's tenacious Get Hoffa Squad, the team was formed

specifically to catch Hoffa. They were relentless in uncovering a pattern of stolen and squandered Union funds,
sweetheart contracts, conflicts of interest among employers and labor leaders, fake paper locals, and rejection of
fair procedures to members. Hoffa became the prime target. In cities across America, physical confrontation
among Unions was a constant threat. Organized crime
associates including gangsters like Bill Bufalino, Angelo
Meli, and Peter Licavoli of the Motor City Detroit; Joey
Glimco and Paul Ricca of Chicago; Babe Triscaro of
Cleveland and Tony "Ducks" Corallo, Vincent Squillante
and Johnny Dio of New York were known to have Union
ties with Hoffa. He never took direct orders from any of
these gangsters, only cues, which made Hoffa even more
dangerous and powerful.

While Jimmy Hoffa was feeling the heat from the
feds, the southern faction of the syndicate remained on his
side. The New York gangsters were aligning themselves
with Frank Fitzsimmons whom they considered a pushover. Hoffa still had Bonanno and Galante in his corner and
made sure he had the southern kingpins. Trafficante and
Marcello were his friends as well. It didn't stay that way
very long as Mafia chiefs in New York began to realize
Hoffa's return to power in the Union could derail their
business interests with the Teamsters. The New York
mobsters were afraid that the Bonanno and Marcello-
Trafficante faction, which had close ties with Hoffa, had
the potential to destroy the so-called American Crime
Syndicate where spheres of influence were closely guard-
ed.

Hoffa wasn't apologetic about the rap sheets of the
men he befriended to accomplish his ambitions. He was
not afraid to speak his mind either. Hoffa once declared to
a national television audience: "Now, when you talk about
the question of hoodlums and gangsters, the first people
who hire hoodlums and gangsters are employers. If there
are any illegal forces in the community he'll use them,
strong-arm and otherwise. And so if you're going to stay
in the business of organizing the unorganized, maintaining
the Union you have, you better have resistance." Hoffa's
resistance comprised of very close alliances with the powerful underworld. With the sensational revelations in upstate New York in 1957, that a secret organized crime
syndicate was operating in the country, an age of inno-
cence came to an end. J. Edgar Hoover's claim that there
was no organized crime in the country was shattered. Attended by over 100 Mafia crime bosses from the United
States, Canada and Italy, the famous Apalachin Meeting
at the home of gangster Joseph Barbara, a soft-drink bot-
tler in upstate New York, brought the Mafia out into the
open. Edgar D. Croswell, a sergeant in the State Police
Bureau of Criminal Investigation, had placed Barbara's
home under occasional surveillance when he suspected
his involvement in three other murders. At an area motel
where Sergeant Croswell had gone to investigate a bad
check case, Croswell noticed Barbara's son making room
reservations. The sergeant then checked with a butcher,
who said Barbara had ordered 200 pounds of steak and
other meat delivered to his mansion. On November 14,
1957, aroused by different license plates on expensive
cars from around the country, Sergeant Croswell, along

with law enforcement on the local and state level swooped down on the meeting, surprising the who's who of the underworld. Many of the Mafiosi, dressed in expensive silk suits, fled into the woods and surrounding area of the Apalachin estate. Over sixty underworld bosses, including Vito Genovese, the reputed head of a New York City crime family, Joseph Profaci, listed by law enforcement officials as a Brooklyn gangster, and Russell Buffalino, reputedly a crime boss in western New York State, were detained and indicted after the botched meeting. The events of that day, much to the embarrassment of FBI boss, forced J. Edgar Hoover to confirm the existence of a National Crime Syndicate.

As the McClellan Committee hearings were getting nationwide attention, a liberal faction of the Mob gained momentum and began to influence and rival the old Mafia power structure. The new group headed by boss Vito Genovese and his allies Carlo Gambino and Gaetano Lucchese decided to snatch control from the Commission and *La Cosa Nostra* outright. By 1957, the unrest was leading to a major war in *La Cosa Nostra*, so Genovese, who controlled the most powerful family in the Syndicate, called for a national meeting of bosses around the country. Genovese ordered Buffalo boss and Commission member Stefan "The Undertaker" Magaddino to organize the meeting. Magaddino, in turn, chose Pennsylvania crime boss Joseph Barbara and his underboss Rosario "Russell" Bufalino to oversee all the arrangements for the meeting known as the infamous "Apalachin Meeting." Bufalino, who was well liked and respected, would later loom large in the events that were to take place eighteen years later when Jimmy Hoffa vanished from the face of the earth in 1975.

After Hoffa's election as president of the International Brotherhood of Teamsters in 1957, he began to solidify his relationship with the Mob. A breakup of the National Crime Syndicate with its traditional spheres of influence was at stake. When Hoffa was in prison at Lewisburg, trouble within the Mob was evident as Hoffa and Tony Provenzano slugged it out after Provenzano accused Hoffa of not giving him a loan for a business he wanted to start. Anthony "Tony Pro" Provenzano was a capo (captain) in the Vito Genovese crime family, which had aligned itself with the New York families opposing Bonanno. Tony Pro Provenzano was a powerful New Jersey Teamster leader and vice president who controlled Teamsters Local 560. Aligning himself with the New York Mafia families that opposed Bonanno, Provenzano was an active participant in the "Banana Wars" as the press called it during the unrest. The New Jersey gangster demanded the Union locals under his jurisdiction to not pay the Bonanno faction, which was on Teamsters payroll. Realizing that Hoffa's release from Lewisburg Prison and his taking back the Union had the potential of stopping access to the pension fund, the Mob wanted to make sure they had the right guy running the Teamsters. They knew Frank Fitzsimmons was an easier mark and favored him as the Teamster boss. Although Frank Fitzsimmons didn't have the influence with Nixon that Hoffa had, he did know John Mitchell, Nixon's attorney general. In 1969, Fitzsimmons and Mitchell met secretly several times while Hoffa was in prison. They came to the conclusion that if Hoffa was released and was allowed to take power over the Union, all hell would break loose. Mitchell, alarmed by the notion that Union warfare could explode all over the country when he promised the American public law and order, put the possibility of freeing Hoffa on the shelf for the time being. For Fitzsimmons, the development was welcome news since he was getting used to being treated with all the fancy perks a Teamster president had.

In 1969, less than three weeks after Nixon took his oath as president, the Mob and Fitzsimmons began to peel away Hoffa's authority and influence by trying to win over his allies. Hoffa was in jail and in no position to counter them. At stake was the massive Union pension funds controlled by Hoffa's friend Allen Dorfman. Dorfman impressed Hoffa enough that he trusted him with the millions of dollars in pension fund resources. Born into a working class family in 1923, Dorfman enlisted in the U.S. Marines after high school and went on to win a Silver Star at the Battle of Iwo Jima. After World War II ended he attended the University of Illinois. His stepfather was Paul "Red" Dorfman, a Chicago-based gangster who led the Chicago Waste Handler's Union and was a kingpin in the Chicago outfit. Alleged ties to organized crime because of his stepfather, dogged Allen Dorfman all his life. Dorfman was eventually indicted, along with several Teamster leaders, for embezzlement from the Union Pension Fund. For several years, it was reputed that Dorfman and Hoffa ran a large-scale program of unsecured loans from Teamsters' pension funds to major figures in organized crime. Dorfman's indictment in 1970, led to a conviction and a one-year prison sentence in federal prison. He was again investigated in 1973 on similar charges related to payoffs.

Hoffa and Dorfman had known each other since 1949. Dorfman formed the Union Insurance Agency and convinced the Teamsters to sign a contract to provide health and welfare insurance for them in the Central States Union. The agreement expanded to accident and sickness insurance that made him a fortune. His relationship with the Union and Hoffa put him in a place of influence and power giving him access to millions of dollars in Teamster pension funds. As the McClellan Committee hearings were nearing its end, Dorfman became a target of an investigation regarding excessive fees paid by the Teamsters to his company. Suspicions that large cash withdrawals from his insurance company were going to Jimmy Hoffa as kickbacks put the Union in an awkward position. Dorfman's power base developed in the late 1950s when he started approving loans for the Teamster's Central States Pension Fund. A large number of the loans were real estate loans to executive Teamster members or to organized crime-connected casinos in Las Vegas. By the late 1950s Hoffa and Dorfman became very close. The unprecedented growth in Teamsters' ranks along with the enormous wealth generated by Union pension contributions was a target for the Mob. Although Dorfman administered the fund, it was Hoffa who decided where the money was going. It wasn't long before the "Get Hoffa Squad" set their sights on Hoffa and how he was using Teamster resources. When Hoffa lost all appeals and entered Lewisburg Prison in 1967, Dorfman took full control of the Central States Teamsters Pension Fund. He may not have been a gangster in the traditional sense but he was crucial to the Mafia's access to huge amounts of money for their various enterprises. Indeed, Dorfman cleverly used his access to the Teamsters' almost limitless pension fund to establish himself as banker to the Mob. It was clear for the FBI. If they snagged Dorfman, they had an opportunity to stop the funneling of money to the Mob. The revelation that Dorfman was a key player in the illegal use of Teamster pension funds sparked the most intense wiretapping operation in U.S. history. Even when the operation was going on, Dorfman got into action authorizing a $160 million loan to a group called Argent Corporation which owned a number of casinos, including the Stardust Resort and Casino. Many of the casinos in Vegas were infiltrated by mobsters who skimmed millions from casino operations that came largely under Dorfman's administration. Allen Dorfman's career came to an end when he was convicted in December of 1982, along with Roy L. Williams, president of the Teamsters, and three others for conspiring to bribe former Senator Howard Canon of Nevada to block a trucking deregulation bill. The federal judge in the case said Dorfman was an "evil manipulator" and promised a long jail term. Armed with Dorfman's conviction and wire taps of Dorfman's private dealings, the government knew it had enough on him to put him away for a long time. Two days before Dorfman's sentencing, scheduled for January 23, 1983, Dorfman was murdered in typical gangland execution style. The murder was presumably intended to keep him from cooperating with the Justice Department.

Dan E. Moldea, author of *The Hoffa Wars*, remembered his first encounter with Allen Dorfman while he was a young crime reporter. "During spring break, when I was in graduate school . . . I wound up going to Chicago for the Gala Products Trial and it was there at the Federal Court House and during a break in the trial that I saw two guys standing outside. Thinking I knew who they were— Irv Weiner and Allen Dorfman—I intruded on their conversation and asked Dorfman about his role with the Mob . . . His response to me was, he was no different and certainly no worse than any banker or businessman who operated in America today. That was his position. He said he was just a business man who deals with large sums of money and did it, in his opinion, in a very legitimate way." Along the way Dorfman became a millionaire—a lodge in Wisconsin, a house in La Costa, California, and a $750,000 home in Chicago Heights made for getaways all over the country. His wealth gave him great power and prestige. A charity named him Man of the Year, but with power came a host of problems. In the 1960s, someone tried to kill him with a shotgun. A star witness against him in the 1970s was killed by a masked gunman. In the 1980s, long after his mentor and friend Jimmy Hoffa disappeared, Dorfman was indicted on extortion charges in the bombing of a former associate's house. His string of luck ran out in a hail of bullets in 1983, but not before scamming over 450,000 Teamsters and their families out of millions of dollars through the pension and welfare funds from 1950 until his death.

The Mob and Teamsters needed somebody they could trust. Allen Dorfman fit the bill to a tee. Respected among all parties and put in control of the Union's pension and welfare funds by Jimmy Hoffa, Dorfman's responsibility was to make sure organized crime got its fair share of the Union's billion-dollar pension and welfare funds. After Richard Nixon was sworn in as President of the United States in 1969 Hoffa was in prison for two years. The time was ripe for Allen Dorfman to become Frank Fitzsimmons' peacemaker and confident. By mid1971Richard Nixon had forced Hoffa to resign all his Union offices in return for a pardon. The action set the stage for Frank Fitzsimmons' election as the International Brotherhood of Teamsters general president in a raucous convention a month later. Little did Hoffa know, Nixon's pardon meant he was barred from Union office until 1980. Organized crime, the White House, and the Teamsters were now closer than ever. Hoffa was the man out and he didn't like it. Almost five years into his 13-year prison term, Hoffa was released from Lewisburg prison on December 23, 1971, after Richard Nixon commuted his sentence. When Hoffa got out, Teamster officials awarded Hoffa a $1.7 million lump sum payment, an unprecedented settlement at the time. Although the former Union boss and now ex-convict was happy to be out of prison, he was enraged with the condition imposed on his release which inhibited his participation in Union activities until March 1980. Hoffa accused Nixon of depriving him of his rights. Earlier in 1971, Hoffa was about to appear before the parole board to plead for an early release. He was getting information from the Nixon administration and from Fitzsimmons that his chance for parole was not good if he still insisted on holding on to the Union presidency. Believing he was being offered a choice—parole in exchange for resigning his office, Hoffa accepted the terms, thinking that once he was out of prison, Fitzsimmons would walk away.

When Hoffa resigned, Fitzsimmons and the Nixon White House were relieved. Fitzsimmons immediately called a special meeting of the Teamsters' executives to declare him president, and two weeks later, at a Teamster convention the majority of delegates elected him for a five-year term. Hoffa was expected to be released by the middle of 1972, and Fitzsimmons still was not feeling safe, thinking Hoffa would move quickly to regain his office. He was getting anxious trying to figure out a way to block Hoffa. Having close ties to the White House, Fitzsimmons discussed his fears with Chuck Colson, Attorney General John Mitchell, and other friends in the administration. In December, they barnstormed a solution. Presidential clemency would be granted to Hoffa but with a stipulation attached that prohibited him from resuming any Union activities for another eight years. Charles "Chuck" Colson, special counsel to President Nixon from 1969 to 1973, was another figure that was involved with the Hoffa case. Known as the hatchet man, Colson gained notoriety at the height of the Watergate scandal when he was named one of the Watergate conspirators. He pleaded guilty to obstruction of justice for attempting to defame Pentagon Papers defendant Daniel Ellsberg. In 1974, he served seven months in federal prison, becoming the first member of the Nixon administration to be jailed for Watergate-related charges. Hoffa was never informed of the conditions for his pardon and when he found out, he was determined to have them overturned. A few years later, White House counsel John Dean claimed that "John Mitchell ordered me to draw up papers and he casually mentioned that Hoffa had agreed not to get involved in the Union. So I said, 'Why not put that into the president's declaration?' He agreed. The whole thing was an afterthought added by us at the very last minute." After Nixon's failed bid for governor of California in 1962, he moved to New York to join Mitchell's law firm. Mitchell was a confidant of Nixon's managing his successful run for president in 1968. Nixon appointed Mitchell attorney general during a period of almost daily civil protest and growing turmoil over the Vietnam War and civil rights movement.

Calling for a tough law-and-order posture, Attorney General Mitchell is credited for swaying deciding votes to put Nixon into the presidency. He described demonstrators in 1969 as "active militants who wanted to destroy the processes and institutions of the government." In a *Washington Post* profile of Mitchell in 1970, Don Oberdorfer wrote, *People have noticed that when Richard M. Nixon utters a declarative sentence, he often turns toward John N. Mitchell as if searching for approval or reassurance. He is without question the most powerful man in the Cabinet.* Mitchell resigned his position of attorney general in 1972 to serve again in Nixon's 1972 presidential campaign. In 1975, Mitchell was found guilty of conspiracy, obstruction of justice and perjury for his role in the Watergate affair. He entered prison in 1977, serving 19 months behind bars. John Mitchell died of a heart attack outside his home at the age of 75 in 1988.

WILLIAM HRYB

CHAPTER TEN

HOFFA COMES BACK

At a Labor Day rally in 1971, President Frank Fitzsimmons for the first time urged President Richard Nixon to pardon Jimmy Hoffa publicly. With no fanfare or media releases, Jimmy Hoffa's attorney, Morris Shenker, filed a petition on December 16, 1971, seeking a pardon for Hoffa from the White House. Usually, a petition has to go through the Department of Justice for a response, followed by input from the FBI, then two sentencing judges are required to review the request. The procedures sometimes take years to process, but in Hoffa's case, the petition was marked "approved" almost immediately by Attorney General John Mitchell. It's no wonder then that *Life* magazine once called Morris Shenker the "foremost lawyer of the Mob in the U.S." Despite his alleged business and personal ties with mobsters, Shenker chaired some important offices.

He was the former head of the St. Louis Commission on Crime and Law Enforcement giving him a high profile. Because of his ties to the Teamsters and alleged Mob connections, Shenker eventually was investigated by the Nevada Gaming Commission. A federal grand jury accused him of conspiring to conceal hundreds of thousands of dollars from the Internal Revenue Service and creditors from 1967 to 1973 while he was involved in bankruptcy proceedings. He vehemently denied the charges and ultimately the charges were dropped. As for Jimmy Hoffa, Richard Nixon signed an Executive Grant of Clemency in record time on December 23, 1971. Hoffa's original thirteen-year sentence was now reduced to six-and-a-half years. With good behavior, the reduced sentence guaranteed Hoffa's immediate release. That same day, he walked out of Lewisburg Penitentiary and boarded a plane that flew him to his daughter Barbara's home in St. Louis for a long-awaited Christmas gathering. The satisfaction of being together with his family for Christmas after four years in prison was a brief respite for a restless Jimmy Hoffa who was planning his comeback. For Hoffa, the end justified the means. Hoffa was prepared to make sure all those who conspired against him would get what they deserved. As he once told Robert Kennedy over dinner, "I do to others what they do to me, only worse." After spending a short time with his family, Hoffa flew back to Detroit for a mandatory registration with the Federal Parole Board and Probation Office. On paper, Hoffa still would be on parole until the six-and-a-half years left in his sentence expired. While in Detroit, Hoffa read the language of the pardon document: *The said James R. Hoffa is not to engage in direct or indirect management of any labor organization prior to March 6, 1980, and if the aforesaid condition is not fulfilled this commutation will be null and void in its entirety.* The stipulation in his pardon was the last straw for a man used to getting his way. Hoffa was more determined than ever to get his position back, no matter what.

After spending some time with his family, Hoffa traveled to Florida for a three-month vacation at his Blair House apartment in Miami Beach. Arriving on January 5, 1972, Hoffa was met at the airport by Frank Ragano, the self-styled Mob lawyer who made his name representing such organized crime figures as Santo Trafficante Jr. and Carlos Marcello. It was a sign of respect from Marcello and Trafficante who could not show their faces knowing that Hoffa could not be seen in the company of organized crime figures or convicted felons. In his 1994 autobiography titled Mob Lawyer, Ragano wrote about his career in defending members of the Mob and made a questionable allegation that the Florida Mafia boss Santo Trafficante Jr. confessed to him shortly before he died in 1987 that he and kingpin Carlos Marcello had arranged the assassination of President John F. Kennedy in 1963. Before Castro overthrew the Battista government in Cuba, Ragano was a frequent visitor to Havana's nightclubs owned by Trafficante. During one visit, Trafficante told Ragano that in 1957, he set up then Senator John F. Kennedy with several whores in a Havana hotel room and that Trafficante regretted not preserving the night with secret surveillance tapes that he could have used to blackmail the soon to be U.S. president. The 1959 Cuban Revolution changed everything for the Mob. Fidel Castro was now in charge and was steadfast in closing down all the Mob's Havana casinos. Trafficante's casinos were the first to be shut down and to make matters worse for the mobster, he was thrown into prison. Thanks to Ragano, Trafficante was released the following year and returned to the U.S. Facing corruption charges from the U.S. Justice Department, Hoffa hired Ragano on Santo Trafficante's recommendations. It was the beginning of an association that would last for years. Using his powerful relationship with Hoffa, Ragano was able to place loans from the Teamsters' Pension Fund in return for finder's fees. Millions of dollars were being funneled as kickbacks to Hoffa from the enormous pension fund. It was like a cash cow ready to be milked anytime the Mob needed money. The activity would go on for more than a decade giving the Mobs their very own bank. Before Hoffa vanished in the summer of 1975, Trafficante asked Ragano to convey an urgent message to Hoffa—"Be very careful and not take any chances." Within days, Hoffa disappeared under mysterious circumstances.

Hoffa's release from prison at the end of 1971 brought intense media attention. In February 1972, Hoffa agreed to appear on ABC's "Issues and Answers," sharing with a wide national audience the news that he would be supporting Richard Nixon for president in the fall. Hoffa's experience told him that he could not trust Nixon's administration to play fair with his parole if he incited them by going after Fitzsimmons. Hoffa was not going to take any chances, so he played it safe by letting Nixon know in a very public way that he was going to support him. One month after the Watergate burglary in July 1972, Frank Fitzsimmons officially endorsed Richard M. Nixon for re-election. As the 1972 presidential campaign approached, Nixon sent Chuck Colson to the Teamsters California La Costa meeting to make sure Nixon had the Teamsters in his pocket. Frank Fitzsimmons and Harold Gibbons, the St. Louis Union leader who was the apparent successor to Hoffa before he named Fitzsimmons to replace him were at each other's throats. Those who were present could hear both men screaming at each other. Gibbons told Fitzsimmons that he had sold out to Nixon and was trying to turn the whole Union over to him. "Under no conditions will I ever endorse Richard Nixon for anything, including dog catcher. You can stick Nixon right up your ass if you expect me to support him." Joe Franko, Hoffa's long-time supporter and friend recalled Gibbons telling him, "Would you believe that shanty Irish son of a bitch wants me to endorse Nixon after what they've been doing? They've sold the fucking International to him and that Colson. I wouldn't trust that bastard as far as you could throw him. Joe, this man is ruining the International Union," Gibbons said. The dissenting vote belonged to Harold Gibbons, the vice president who infuriated Hoffa when he lowered the Teamster flag to half-staff in honor of the death of John Kennedy almost a decade earlier. Fitzsimmons didn't care what Gibbons thought and endorsed Nixon for president. As an award for Fitzsimmon's patronage, Nixon appointed the Union leader's wife, Patricia Fitzsimmons, to serve on the Arts Committee of the Kennedy Center for Performing Arts. Hoffa was getting ready for the fight of his life. His plan of attack centered on the legal challenge to the condition of his pardon. His civil-rights legal team would argue that the president exceeded his authority by adding a condition to his pardon. Lawyers for Hoffa pointed out that under the US Constitution a president has the ability to pardon or not pardon, but he has no power to pardon in such a way that his pardon could later be thrown out and the recipient returned to jail. The basic argument was that a conditional pardon would give a president more power than the Founding Fathers intended him to have. The condition imposed on Hoffa was deemed by his lawyers as being an added punishment because he was not allowed to manage a Union.

Hoffa had no such restriction in prison; even though jail rules made it difficult to operate, it was not forbidden. When he was sentenced to the thirteen years in jail, no conditional punishment was imposed and the president did not have the power to increase a punishment handed down by the sentencing judge. Hoffa and his lawyers also believed this condition violated his First Amendment right of freedom of speech and of assembly by putting off-limits, a valid and legitimate forum for exercise of these freedoms. Hoffa loathed prison and wanted to get out of prison as soon as possible. He was afraid Nixon might rescind his parole if he filed a lawsuit, so he decided to keep quiet until his parole expired and went "off paper" in March, 1973.

Charles Colson, who was a special counsel to Nixon and in charge of his "enemy list," loomed large in being complicit in the issue of Hoffa's restriction. Dean testified that Colson ordered him to initiate an IRS investigation into the finances of Harold Gibbons, the only Teamster member of the executive board who did not vote to endorse Nixon for re-election. During the Watergate investigation, a memo from Colson to Dean was produced requesting an audit and calling Gibbons an "all-out enemy." In a deposition, Hoffa testified, "I blame one man for the restriction on my pardon, Charles Colson." Colson would take the Fifth Amendment on the subject during the Watergate hearings, although he did admit talking about the pardon with Fitzsimmons before Nixon granted it. After Colson resigned from the White House, he went into private practice. Fitzsimmons, in a clearly motivated decision, took the International Brotherhood of Teamsters legal contract from Edward Bennett Williams and gave it to Charles Colson, ensuring him of a $100,000 minimum retainer per year. Williams had gained a reputation of being a Mob lawyer. In the 1950s he was hired by Mob boss Frank Costello who had been convicted of income tax evasion. After Williams managed to get Costello released from prison, he said, "I've had forty lawyers, but Ed is the champ." Links with the underworld was reinforced when Williams started working for Hoffa in the early 1960s and helped to acquit him of the charge of accepting an illegal payment from an employer. Robert Kennedy later claimed if it wasn't for Williams he would have put Hoffa away a lot sooner. When Hoffa was granted parole, he was not going to take any chances that Nixon might overturn his pardon and put him back in jail. In his autobiography he wrote, *I spent fifty-eight months in Lewisburg and I can tell you this on a stack of Bibles: prisons are archaic, bru-*

*tal, unregenerative, overcrowded hell holes where the in-
mates are treated like animals with absolutely not one
humane thought given to what they are going to do once
they are released. You're like an animal in a cage and
you're treated like one.*

When Hoffa got out of prison he had to get permission
to travel anywhere. He was not allowed to go to Union
conferences but he was permitted to go to cities around
the country for other reasons. At Union gatherings, he
would stay in the same hotel as the other Union members
and would hold court with Union members in hotel lob-
bies. Hoffa was doing a lot of under-the-table campaigning, including calling members around the country on the
telephone. His strategy was to let everyone know that he
intended to come back and to make sure they were not
going over to Fitzsimmons. Hoffa was sure he'd have the
Union's support but he had a vindictive streak and was
determined to get even with Fitzsimmons and "Tony Pro"
Provenzano. Hoffa and Tony Pro had been allies in the
"brass knuckles" days when Hoffa was shaping the Teamsters into the country's biggest and most powerful Union.
Provenzano was born on May 7, 1917, on the Lower East
Side of Manhattan to poor Sicilian immigrants. The Genovese crime family capo was the vice president of the
100,000 strong Teamsters Local 560 in Union City, New
Jersey. With Jimmy Hoffa's blessing, the slight 5'7", 155-
pound gangster cleverly used his position to steal funds
for his personal use. Hoffa had no illusions about the
Mob. He knew he needed them and to solidify his support
among Mob elite, Hoffa emboldened the Mafia's heavy-
hitters who were associated with the Teamsters to use

their locals as personal bank accounts. The two became bitter enemies after Hoffa insulted Provenzano, telling him, "It's because of people like you that I got into trouble in the first place." Tony Pro served four years of a seven-year stretch for extortion. After Hoffa and Provenzano were released from prison, they allegedly had a violent confrontation at a chance meeting in an airport. In his book *Desperate Bargain: Why Jimmy Hoffa Had to Die*, author Lester Velie wrote, *Hoffa and Provenzano went at it with their fists, and Hoffa broke a bottle over Provenzano's head. Provenzano vowed he would retaliate against Hoffa's grandchildren, saying, "I'll tear your heart out!"* A month after Hoffa vanished, Tony Provenzano told a reporter at his Florida home, "As much as I love the guy, Jimmy became an egotistical maniac. It's bad for a guy when he doesn't know how to take a loss." Then speaking of himself, "I'm a human being, I just want to be left alone . . . I don't do anything abnormal. I'm not a faggot. My great joy is my family." Tony Pro Provenzano was photographed in a golfing outing with former President Richard Nixon within a year after Jimmy Hoffa's disappearance. The media were all over the story, especially when Provenzano was being linked to Hoffa's disappearance. In 1978, Provenzano was convicted of the 1961 murder of Anthony Castellito whose body was never found either with rumors that his body was destroyed by a tree shredder. Tony Pro ended up going to prison and died in the prison hospital on December 12, 1988, of a heart attack at the age of 71. When Frank Fitzsimmons became the president of the International Brotherhood of Teamsters, many of Hoffa's supporters had shifted their loyalty to the new Union boss. Roy Williams, a high ranking Teamster official who later became the president of the Teamster's after Fitzsimmons' death, asked for advice from Joseph Franco who was Hoffa's old friend. In their book, *Hoffa's Man*, authors Richard Hammer and Joseph Franko wrote, *Your loyalty has got to be with the boss and right now, Fitz is the boss. If Jimmy tells you to do anything other than that, just tell him in his own language that whoever is the head of the Teamsters, that's where your loyalty goes to, no matter whether you like him or not. You've got him and that's it, and you're stuck with him. But you respect Jimmy and you give him loyalty, but you're a Teamster, number one. If he tries to put you in the middle, you tell him, 'Jim, I love you. I love you as a friend, but please don't ask me to go against Fitz out in the open.' That's what he did and I think Jimmy respected him for it because there was always a good feeling between Jim and Roy all the way to the end.* As stubborn and bull-headed as he was, Hoffa did not like it but he understood that a lot of Teamster officials had to put on a public show of loyalty to Fitzsimmons if they were to keep their positions. Hoffa felt as long as they kept in touch and supported him in private, he would tolerate their public backing of Fitzsimmons.

The road to re-capturing the presidency of the Teamsters would be long and Hoffa knew it. His son, James Jr., told Joe Franco, "Joe, I wish you would go out and see dad and sit down with him. He's driving mother absolutely crazy. He just sits there and raves all day long. He's going to kill her. I wish to God my father never goes back to the Teamsters. I think mother and the rest of the family have had just enough of it. If he goes back, we're going to have to go through the whole thing again, and it's going to be worse. We've just had enough. If you could talk dad into doing something else and stop what he's doing, I'd be grateful." Franco said, "Jim, there's no way you can tell your dad to stop. You know he wants to be head of the Teamsters and there's no way of stopping him." James Jr. responded, "I know it. He's like a raving maniac. But I really feel sorry for my mother. Every time anything comes down, she got the brunt of it."

As Hoffa was gaining strength from the rank and, Chuckie O'Brien deserted him for Fitzsimmons. O'Brien was like an adopted son whom Hoffa took care of when O'Brien's mother was left a widow. His mother was a friend of Josephine Hoffa, and when O'Brien decided school was not for him, Hoffa put him on the payroll as a business agent for Teamsters Local 299 and Teamster organizer. After Hoffa's release from jail, O'Brien recognized that Fitzsimmons had the power now, and Hoffa's chances of regaining the Union was slim. A $40,000 per year salary he was getting from the Teamsters trumped any loyalty and gratitude he had for Hoffa. O'Brien was all for Fitzsimmons, especially when he found there was a Union job in Florida that might be available. Hoffa would never forgive O'Brien for betraying him.

Stubbornly, Hoffa was convinced the Union wanted him back. Many of his former allies, including Fitzsimmons, started to get worried and feared what Hoffa might do if he got back into office. The Mob, which was riding on Fitzsimmons' generosity, was especially worried that their cash cow Union pension fund would dry up. In the summer of 1975, a war was shaping up between Hoffa and Fitzsimmons. Worst of all, the gangsters who had relied on Teamster pension money for decades were now in danger of losing access to easy money.

CHAPTER ELEVEN

HOFFA DISAPPEARS

"**M**y father, James R. Hoffa, has been missing for some thirty-two hours. He left for an appointment at Machus Red Fox Restaurant at approximately 1 p.m. on Wednesday, July 30th. He called home approximately 2:15 p.m.—and we have not heard from him since." Those were the chilling words spoken by James Hoffa Jr. to reporters, a day after the infamous Union boss went mysteriously missing in 1975. That summer, Hoffa called his wife from a pay phone outside a restaurant in Oakland County Michigan. It was the last time his family would hear from him. Jimmy Hoffa's appointment that day was with two men widely reported to be reputed members of the Detroit and New Jersey Mafia. This has led many to conclude that he was likely killed by the Mob.

More than two hundred FBI agents were assigned to investigate Jimmy Hoffa's disappearance. A grand jury was convened and more than 16,000 pages worth of reports were written. But his fate remains a mystery. A cold case. Hoffa was declared legally dead in 1982; however, the FBI did not stop digging literally or figuratively for his remains. From 2003 to 2013, FBI agents picked up shovels and combed through dirt and mud searching for the remains or hints of Hoffa's disappearance. Agents have dug up a horse farm, a shed, an underground pool, and most recently on June 18 and 19, in a field in Oakland Township outside Detroit. Former Detroit Mafia capo Tony Zerilli tipped off the FBI with a claim that Hoffa's remains were buried in a small field surrounded by trees and a gravel road. Armed with a backhoe, more than 40 FBI agents spent over 20 hours for two days digging before calling it quits. "Certainly, we're disappointed," Detroit FBI Chief Robert Foley told reporters on Wednesday June 19, 2013, as federal and local authorities wrapped up another excavation that failed to turn up anything that could be linked to Hoffa. The mystery of what happened to the best known Union boss in the United States is likely to remain Michigan's best kept secret.

"I'm here...to let you know that after a diligent search pursuant to our responsibility under the search warrant, we did not uncover any evidenced relevant on the investigation of James R. Hoffa," a disappointed Robert Foley commented at the site. "We are always hopeful that we'll get a lead that will lead us to a position which we can conclude this investigation, both for the process of justice and the family." Almost four months before Hoffa vanished into thin air in 1975, the rumors at a Teamster convention that spring was that Hoffa was talking and cooperating with the FBI. A story written in the *Detroit Free Press* in 1992 credited the rumors to Chuckie O'Brien, Hoffa's so-called adopted son and alleged driver of the deep maroon 1975 Mercury Marquis which Hoffa was in at the time of his disappearance. In a FBI file on Hoffa called the HOFFEX file, item 302 confirms the existence of this rumor and the believable reason why it may have had some credibility. The FBI issued a statement saying, "It has been rumored among sources that Hoffa, while attempting to gain control of the Teamsters, may have provided information to the government in exchange for a favorable decision concerning his Union restrictions." Memos in the HOFFEX file are haunting:

- On May 15, 1975, Jimmy Hoffa testified at a grand jury investigation into "no show" jobs at his former Detroit Local 299. Hoffa took the Fifth. Afterward, when questioned by a reporter, Hoffa said he was "damn proud of it." That same Jimmy Hoffa attended a meeting at his son's law office with his son and Detroit mobster Anthony "Tony Jack" Giacalone. Giacalone tried to broker a meeting between Hoffa and "Tony Pro" Provenzano, and Hoffa refused to attend. Giacalone then asked for Hoffa's help in obtaining records that were going to be used by the government against Giacalone for an alleged insurance scam indictment. Hoffa turned down Giacalone's request.

- At the end of May, Frank Fitzsimmons threatened to put Local 326, Hoffa's former local and power base, into trusteeship and have it run by a monitor who would report to the Teamsters' headquarters in Washington.

- On June 19, 1975, Jimmy Hoffa's ally and good friend Sam Giancana was assassinated in his Chicago home five days before his scheduled testimony before the Church Committee on the Mob's role in a CIA plot to assassinate Fidel Castro.

- On June 25, 1975, a Local 299 supporter of Frank Fitzsimmons named Ralph Proctor was attacked from behind as he walked out a restaurant after lunch. Proctor never saw what hit him. Proctor was beaten and knocked unconscious in broad daylight. Proctor's higher-up in the Fitzsimmons camp, Rolland McMaster, said, "We had that kind of crap happen; I put investigators on it, but they didn't find out anything."

- On the afternoon of July 10, 1975, Frank Fitzsimmons' son Richard Fitzsimmons relaxed in Nemo's bar in Detroit. Richard was vice president of Local 299, and in that capacity he had been finishing his last drink at Nemo's. Richard left the bar and was walking toward this parked Lincoln when the car exploded. Richard narrowly escaped being injured, but his white Lincoln was blown to bits.

- On the afternoon of July 30, 1975, Jimmy Hoffa disappeared.

What happened that summer day almost forty years ago is still a mystery, but a plausible sketch can be examined from police records, justice department archives, journalists' reports and the general public. That morning Jimmy Hoffa was sitting at home, sipping coffee and going over papers in his den when he received a telephone call. The caller asked Hoffa to come to a meeting at the Red Fox Restaurant, which was a few miles from his home. Hoffa was to meet with Anthony "Tony Pro" Provenzano, an important kingpin in a New Jersey Teamsters Local, and Anthony "Tony Jack" Giacalone, a reputed Mafia capo from Detroit, at 2:00 p.m. that afternoon. Hoffa believed he could settle some differences and continue his fight to regain the Teamsters' presidency. Little did he know, later that day Hoffa would never be seen again. Apparently the caller was "Tony Jack" Giacalone whose motive was to make peace between the two.

Anthony Provenzano and Hoffa knew each other from the old days when they were organizers for the Union. Both were tough and ruled with an iron fist. If anybody crossed these guys, they would pay the consequences fast. While Provenzano was in prison for extortion, he watched out for his old friend; but things went sour when they began to quarrel and their friendship ended. Anthony "Tony Pro" Provenzano was vice president of Teamsters Local 560 in Union City and president of the New Jersey Area Joint Council under Jimmy Hoffa. Tony Pro was a former fighter, Union organizer and truck driver. *Time* magazine called the ill-tempered gangster the "Ruler of Newark docks." He had special skills like tampering with the Teamster pension funds and using the money for various Genovese family schemes, such as the one to create kickbacks from a deal with Saint Barnabas Hospital which needed funding for their new hospital in the suburbs. A recent declassified document released by the FBI stated that Eugene Catena assisted Hoffa and Tony Pro to facilitate a Teamsters' loan offer of $750 million to the medical center. The loan would have paid Hoffa and Provenzano $750,000 in kickbacks. Provenzano, an immediate suspect in the disappearance of Jimmy Hoffa in 1975, was convicted of ordering the murder of Anthon Castilleto three years later in 1978. Castilleto was a rival local member who went up against Tony during Union elections. Provenzano's hand-picked enforcer, Harry Konigsberg, an extortionist, was arrested and convicted of carrying out the murder of the prime witness to the hit. The powerful Union boss and mobster was the FBI's prime suspect in the disappearance of Jimmy Hoffa in 1975. After establishing an alibi in the Hoffa case—he was in the company of Union leaders in Hoboken when the former Teamster boss vanished off the face of the earth—Tony Pro took a break at his Hallandale, Florida, home entertaining a reporter from People magazine. Tony Pro died of a heart attack at the age of seventy-one in 1988, while serving time in prison for the Castilleto murder.

Jimmy Hoffa was a driven man while trying to unseat Frank Fitzsimmons. Hoffa buzzed the campaign trail accusing Fitzsimmons of selling out to the mobsters and letting known racketeers into the Teamsters. In Hoffa's autobiography, which was scheduled to be released six months before the 1976 election, Hoffa wrote, I charge him with permitting underworld establishment of a Union insurance scheme. There will be more developments as time goes on and I get my hands on additional information. At the time of his comeback, Hoffa had an interest in a coal mine in northeastern Pennsylvania. To avoid the appearance of having his own conflict of interest, he divested himself out of his coal mining interests. The perception of him having a company role just didn't fit-in, especially when he was pointing his finger at Fitzsimmons' relationship with the underworld. Hoffa was a man obsessed, "If it takes a million, if it takes two million, whatever it takes, I'll buy every political son of a bitch that had anything to do with that deal." Hoffa was still livid over the "deal" that Nixon and Fitzsimmons made in keeping Hoffa out of Union activities until 1980. Two weeks before Hoffa disappeared, he asked his long-time friend Joe Franco to come over to his cottage outside Detroit. "I'm getting John Dean to tell the truth. I'm getting John Mitchell to tell the truth, and I'm getting that drunken bitch of a wife of his. But that Colson and the man that used to sit in the big chair in the Oval Office before they got him, they're the ones that fucked me, and I'll fuck them before I'm done!" Hoffa screamed. "When we get back in, we're gonna clean the house. They'll need to follow me around with a fucking meat wagon. I got a list and they're gonna go. Number one on that list is that fucking Irishman (Fitzsimmons). Franco, I'm going to ask you to do something I never asked you to do before. I want you to hit Fitz." Joe Franco began to say something but Hoffa was on a rant. "Number two is Bobby Holmes. That son of a bitch, that English bastard. I'll tell you something, I'll do him myself. Just wait until I get back in office. And number three is Dusty Miller. I made the motherfucker. I took him from nothing and made him an International organizer. I made him an International vice president and he dumped me and went with Fitz. And that fucking little bastard, Chuckie O'Brien. I brought that kid here from

Kansas City because his mother wanted him here, and I
raised him like he was my own, and let him tell people
that he's like my adopted son. That little son of a bitch,
he's got nothing to do with me. I did it out of respect for
his father and his mother. I did everything for that kid."
Joe Franco tried to calm him down, "Hey, Jimmy, you
don't have to tell me that. Everybody knows that." Hoffa
shot back: "Go to hell, Franco. Look at what he's done.
He kissed and made up in bed with Fitz for a stinking
job." Franco was sure Chuck O'Brien would apologize to
Jimmy when he got in as president. "He's a kid and I'm
sure Chuckie loves you because I've talked to him, and he
feels bad about it because you pissed him off." Hoffa did
not want any part of the explanation. "I don't want to hear
that shit, that little cocksucker. If I ever catch him, I'll
beat his fucking brains out, the two-faced bastard. Just let
me see and he won't know what hit him. All of them, I
made all of them, I did everything for all of them, they
wouldn't be shit if it wasn't for me, and all of them are
just sticking the knife in my back. They got to go. There's
no two ways about it." Franco looked at Hoffa and said, "I
can't do it, Jimmy . . . I can't do what you ask . . . I ain't
gonna hit Fitz."

With no trace of Jimmy Hoffa and the media clamor-
ing for information on his disappearance, the government
started issuing reports about six months after he vanished.
Police authorities revealed that they interviewed Ralph
Picardo who was serving a sentence in Trenton State Pris-
on for murder and claimed he knew what happened to
Jimmy Hoffa. Picardo was a former business agent for
Local 84 in New Jersey and a former driver for Tony Pro

Provenzano. Dan E. Moldea, author of *The Hoffa Wars*, later wrote that Picardo claimed that Hoffa was invited to the Machus Red Fox restaurant by Detroit mobster Anthony Giacalone for a "sit-down" with Provenzano. Chuckie O'Brien told the police that he spent time carving a large fish that day, picked up Hoffa at the restaurant and took him to a nearby house where he was staying with friends. According to Picardo, there were three guys: Thomas Andretta, a Teamster business agent, and Salvatore Briguglio and his brother, Gabriel, who waited in the house to ambush Hoffa. In the sensational claim, Picardo told police that Bufalino ordered the hit on Hoffa and gave the contract to Tony Pro Provenzano.

WILLIAM HRYB

CHAPTER TWELVE

WHAT HAPPENED ON JULY 30, 1975

Rosa Rio "Russell" Bufalino looms large in the Jimmy Hoffa case. There is no other crime figure that compares to the little known gangster who built his empire over six decades from Prohibition to the Jimmy Carter presidency. Bufalino was born in Sicily in 1903 and emigrated to the United States through Ellis Island in 1914. His remarkable rise from a Sicilian immigrant to a Mafia soldier to Mob kingpin defies imagination. A United States Senate subcommittee in 1964 claimed he was "one of the most ruthless and powerful Mob leaders in America." Bufalino's Mob life saga spans over six decades, with relatively little mentioned about him in the media. The FBI file on the mobster known as

"McGee" by his friends paints a compelling case that Bufalino's unpretentious and quiet life in Kingston, Pennsylvania, a beautiful tree-line community of 13,000, obscured a criminal career of nationwide significance. Over a 30-year period FBI records show a direct link to Bufalino and his crime family to bookmaking, stolen goods, loansharking, Union racketeering, narcotics and related violence. Feared by fellow mobsters, feted by politicians, and dogged by federal prosecutors, Bufalino was a driving force in American crime history.

Charles Brandt, a former Delaware state prosecutor and author of *I Heard You Paint Houses* said, "He was one of the most powerful Mob bosses of his day, if not of all time." Former Teamster official and self-proclaimed hitman, Frank Sheeran, is the subject of Brandt's 2004 stunning book chronicling Sheeran's life and his admission that he was the trigger-man to Jimmy Hoffa's murder on orders from Russell Bufalino. Frank Sheeran lived a unique and exciting life. A combat-hardened hero of World War II, Sheeran was born in 1920 to a working class Philadelphia family of Irish and Swedish descent. He enlisted in 1941 and was assigned to the military police before transferring to the 45th Infantry Division known as The Thunderbirds. While in the army he grew to his full adult height of 6 feet 4 inches and was cited for serving 411 days of combat duty (the average was 100) becoming a hardened killing machine. He told his biographer, Charles Brandt, "When an officer would tell you to take a couple of German prisoners back behind the line, and for you to 'hurry back,' you did what you had to do." After the war, Frank "the Irishman" Sheeran found a job as a truck driver, becoming a Teamster; and to make extra money, he started committing loan sharking and other crimes. He soon caught the attention of Russell Bufalino. Sheeran, a man who put his violent side to good use fighting Germans during the war was now well trained ideally to become an enforcer and hit man who worked closely with the reclusive Pennsylvania Mob boss. Rising quickly within the ranks of the Teamsters Union, Sheeran asked Bufalino to introduce him to Jimmy Hoffa. The friendship developed into a trusting relationship and lasted until Bufalino assigned him the task of dealing with the former Union leader. In a civil RICO suit, Rudy Giuliani, a former prosecutor and ex-mayor of New York, accused Sheeran of "acting in concert" with *La Cosa Nostra*'s ruling commission— one of only two non-Italians on Guiliani's list of twenty-six top Mob figures which included the sitting bosses of the Bonnano, Genovese, Colombo, Lucchese, Chicago and Milwaukee families, as well as various underbosses. Sheeran did not like the notoriety, but it showed how important he was in the feds' attack on organized crime.

When Hoffa got out of prison, he was a changed man. There was only one thing on his mind, and that was to get the presidency of the Teamsters Union back; and he didn't care how he did it. Many believed Hoffa was becoming reckless by telling the press that he was going to expose the Mob and was going to clean-house. His crucial mistake was letting it be known that the Mob was not going to come close to the Teamster Pension Fund. For Hoffa to say this was hypocritical, because it was he who brought the Mob into the Union in the first place.

111

With Teamster elections fast approaching, in 1976 Hoffa began angling to reclaim his old job from former lieutenant Frank Fitzsimmons in a big way, filing suit with the federal government to lift the ban against his taking an active role with the Union. Even if the gambit fizzled—and success looked grim—Hoffa believed that President Gerald Ford was unlikely to push the panic button and throw him back into prison if he broke the terms of his pardon. Richard Nixon resigned in disgrace in August of 1974 because of the Watergate Scandal, and his vice president, Gerald Ford, was sworn into office. With U.S. presidential primaries only six months away, Hoffa figured that Ford would not risk alienating his followers among the Teamster rank and file. In the meantime, Fitzsimmons-versus-Hoffa factional violence reared its ugly head at the Detroit local: its president's boat had been blown up, its vice president's car had been dynamited, and an organizer had been badly beaten up.

A few days before Hoffa disappeared, Frank Sheeran asked his boss and mentor, Russell "McGee" Bufalino, if he could call Hoffa at his cottage near Lake Orion outside Detroit. You needed permission from the big boss himself to make any overtures of peace, especially when Hoffa was threatening to blow the cover on his Mob friends. Things were heating up fast and it was only a matter of time before Bufalino had enough of Hoffa's bluster and would do what the Mob always did to get rid of a problem. Sheeran was worried for his friend and wanted to convince Hoffa to drop the idea of coming back into the Union and it had to be quick. Just nine months earlier at Frank Sheeran's "appreciation night," Jimmy Hoffa flew to Philadelphia to be the featured speaker at the Latin Casino. Over 3,000 friends including Russell Bufalino, Mayor Rizzo, the district attorney, his old war day buddies, and members of the underworld were in attendance. The FBI were keeping a close eye on who was coming and going for future reference. Singer Jerry Vale sang Bufalino's favorite song, "Spanish Eyes," out of respect for the Philly Don making it known to everyone present that there was someone very special in the audience.

Russell Bufalino controlled upstate Pennsylvania and large parts of New York, New Jersey and Florida. Since he was based outside New York City, Bufalino was not in the inner circle of the New York families. However, the families came to him for advice on everything. When they needed something important done, they gave the job to Bufalino. The old man was so respected that when Albert Anastasia was murdered in the barber's chair in New York, they made Russell Bufalino the acting head of that family until they could get everything back to normal. Before he gave his speech, Hoffa presented Sheeran with a gold watch encircled with diamonds. Looking out into the big crowd, he said, "I never realized you were that strong." Sheeran beamed at the comment from one of two greatest men he ever met. The other was Russell Bufalino who was seated at a dinner table in front of the dais. Bufalino presented Sheeran with a special gold ring he had made for only three people: himself, his underboss, and Frank "the Irishman" Sheeran. The night before the testimonial dinner, Bufalino and Sheeran met at Broadway Eddie's where he told Sheeran outright that Hoffa should stop running for Union president. He made it clear that Frank Fitzsimmons was their choice to head the Union and any change would jeopardize access to the enormous Teamster Pension Fund for the easy loans they could get. Bufalino made no bones about the fact Fitzsimmons was not difficult to deal with, unlike Hoffa, who got his take under the table but always on his terms. It was not a secret that Fitzsimmons was happy to be the head of the Union basically in a ceremonial role. The Mob felt all he cared about was golfing and drinking and he was the perfect person to be in control of a billion-dollar pension fund.

Hoffa and Bufalino had a sit-down. "What are you running for? You don't need the money," Bufalino asked.

"It's not about the money. I'm not letting Fitz have the Union."

After the dinner Bufalino took Sheeran aside, "Talk to your friend . . . tell him what it is." The simple statement was in fact a death threat. Sheeran was in charge of taking Hoffa back to his hotel after the testimonial and told him that if he didn't change his mind about quitting his bid for the presidency of the Union, he had better get some bodyguards to protect him. "I'm not going that route, or they'll go after my family," Hoffa said.

"Still in all, you don't want to be out on the street by yourself," Sheeran replied.

"Nobody scares Hoffa. I'm going after Fitz, and I'm going to win this election."

"You know what this means . . . Russell himself told me to tell you what it is."

"They wouldn't dare!" Hoffa angrily replied. Sheeran later recalled that Hoffa didn't scare easily, but the discussion he had with Bufalino made its mark and he could see a chink in his armor. It was only a matter of time. Sheeran got the green light to speak to Hoffa and on Sunday, July 27, 1975, he was hoping he would change Hoffa's mind about running for president of the Union while he still had a chance. According to Sheeran, he told Hoffa he would be coming to Detroit with Russell Bufalino to celebrate a wedding for his cousin, Bill Bufalino's daughter. Bill Bufalino was the Teamster's lawyer in Detroit. "There's widespread concern that things are getting out of hand," Sheeran told Hoffa.

"I got ways to protect myself, I got records put away," Hoffa said.

"Please, Jimmy, even my friend is concerned." Sheeran's comment was a reference to Bufalino who gave Sheeran permission to call Hoffa and give him the warning that taking back the Union was not in the cards. "From day one, Hoffa wanted to work this fucking thing out," Hoffa yelled over the phone to Sheeran.

"Jimmy, I know you know this matter's got to be settled. It can't go on like this. I know you're doing a lot of puffing about exposing this and exposing that. I know you're not serious. Jimmy Hoffa's no rat and he never will be a rat, but there is concern. People don't know how you puff."

"The hell Hoffa's not serious. Wait till Hoffa gets back in and gets his hands on the Union records, we'll see if I'm puffing," Hoffa exclaimed.

"Look at the matter last month, Jimmy. That gentleman in Chicago, I'm quite certain everybody thought he was untouchable, including himself. Irresponsible talk that could have hurt certain important friends of ours was his problem." The gentleman Sheeran was referring to was Hoffa's good friend Sam "Momo" Gianacana, the notorious Mob boss who was gunned down before he was to testify at the Church Committee on the CIA-Mob involvement in the Bay of Pigs fiasco and the plot to poison Fidel Castro.

On the day of Hoffa's disappearance and most likely the last day of his life, police say he fired up his green two-door 1974 Pontiac and left his two-storied cottage style home near Orion Lake about 40 miles north of Detroit early that afternoon. Dressed in blue pants and a blue pullover shirt, he told his wife he was going to meet with two colleagues at the Machus Red Fox restaurant in Bloomfield Township, a town northwest of Detroit suburb and would be home about four o'clock just in time to grill steaks for dinner. Hoffa was no stranger to the Red Fox and enjoyed its food and atmosphere so much that the restaurant hosted the wedding reception for his son, James Hoffa Jr., who, at the time, was a Teamsters' lawyer. On his way to the meeting, he supposedly stopped at the offices of Airport Service Lines, a limo service, to see Louis Linteau, the known owner and one-time officer of a Teamster Local in Pontiac, a city not far from Detroit. Linteau had lost his job at the limo service because of an embezzlement conviction, and Hoffa helped him out when he got out of Lewisburg. The employees told Hoffa that Linteau was out to lunch so he waited a while. He told the workers he was going to the Red Fox Inn for a meeting and wanted Linteau to come with him. Hoffa waited for Linteau as long as he could, but it was getting close to his meeting time at the restaurant, so he got in his car and drove off.

Hoffa arrived at the Red Fox early for the 2 p.m. meeting. He never was late for anything and hated to be kept waiting. When nobody showed up after nearly half an hour, he called Linteau who had returned from lunch and told him, "The bastards are late." According to the investigators, Hoffa then telephoned his wife to tell her he was stood up and was going to hang around a little bit longer just in case they showed up. According to the authorities, the two men were not only late, they had no intention of showing up: Tony "Pro" Provenzano apparently was in New Jersey playing cards at his local and the other, Tony "Jack" Giacalone, was getting a massage and haircut at a Detroit athletic club. After calling his wife from a payphone, Hoffa returned to his car and waited. Later, in a statement to police, two people who were at Red Fox restaurant said they saw Hoffa standing by his two-door green Pontiac at approximately 2:30 p.m. when a late model maroon Mercury or Lincoln drove up. The bystanders told police there were three men inside. The encounter appeared to be friendly and after a brief conversation Hoffa got into their car and drove off. The FBI theorized that once in the car, Hoffa was knocked unconscious and either shot or strangled during the trip away from the restaurant. Later that afternoon his body was disposed of in an incinerator and his ashes discarded where they could never be found or detected. At least, that is the generally accepted explanation of events on July 30, 1975, expounded by journalists and circulated by the FBI, the Justice Department, and other investigative branches.

Joseph Franco, Hoffa's old friend, debunks what generally is accepted and theorizes something more sinister happened that day, and it was not the Mob who was responsible for Hoffa's disappearance. Over a decade had passed since Hoffa disappeared, and in a tell-all book with *New York Times* reporter and award-winning author Richard Hammer, Franco describes a man he served loyally for over thirty years. Their book titled *Hoffa's Man*, published in 1987, provides an in-depth look at Hoffa and reveals what he believes happened to him July 30, 1975. Joseph Franco was a business agent in Hoffa's Detroit Teamsters Local and strong-arm for him, coercing non-Union members to sign up and on occasion blowing up the facilities of troublesome employers. Soon after Hoffa was sent to prison in 1967 for jury tampering charges, Franco went to the slammer as well on unrelated labor law charges. In the book, Franco writes, *Jimmy would never have told Josie where he was going or whom he was going to meet. That wasn't his way.* It was Franco's contention that Josie would have accepted not being told where Hoffa was going and would have been "shocked" if he had told her. In addition, Hoffa was supposed to have stopped on the way to his meeting at the Red Fox to see his friend, Louis Linteau, whom he had given money to become the owner of an airport limo business where he was working before getting sent to prison. Franco is further quoted as saying, *Now if Jimmy stopped there and Louis wasn't there, the last thing in the world Jimmy would have done was to go in and talk to some employees, some flunkies, and tell them, 'I've got a meeting over at the Red Fox and I'm meeting with important people,' and naming them. Anybody who knows Jimmy knew that is bullshit....He would not disclose his personal business to anyone.* Franco figures Hoffa would never have stopped off anywhere. A stickler for punctuality, Hoffa would have waited no more than fifteen minutes, and the only reason he might have waited longer was *not because he was waiting for someone to 'mend fences' but because he was waiting for someone to come with information he wanted. The men in the maroon car who purportedly were known to Hoffa and were observed by bystanders is hogwash,* according to Franco. In the book *Hoffa's Man,* Franco described what he observed that hot summer day on July 30, 1975, and it was not intended for his eyes or for the eyes of anyone who knew Hoffa. Franco claimed he spotted people who looked like federal agents hustling Hoffa into their car the day he vanished. *New York Times* reporter Richard Hammer, co-author of *Hoffa's Man,* candidly writes in the introduction that the stories have the "ring of truth." On the day in question, Franco had stopped at the Red Fox shopping center on his way to a meeting in Flint, Michigan, when he spotted Jimmy Hoffa. According to Franco, "Hoffa was standing and walking around near his car like a bantam rooster," *Franco did not want Hoffa to see him because he would think he was spying on him, so he stayed far enough away that Hoffa could not make out who he was. Hoffa looked like he was waiting for someone to deliver documentation he was expecting about his lawsuit against the feds.* Hoffa had been banned from Union activities until 1980 as per the terms and conditions of his pardon from President Nixon. The documentation referred to by Franco was to get the restrictions against Hoffa lifted.

Franco then describes a black four-door Ford LTD carrying an Afro-American and two Caucasian men wearing sport jackets and shirts and ties who looked like federal marshals. After two of the men got out and flashed what appeared to be badges, Hoffa got into the back seat and they drove off in the direction of the Pontiac airport. It was Franco's belief that Hoffa was put on a plane and thrown out over the Great Lakes.

When authorities started to investigate the disappearance of Hoffa, Franco was called to the grand jury five times but he insisted on immunity.

After Hoffa vanished, a lot of theories in what happened that day were being talked about. None are so compelling as Charles Brandt and Frank Sheeran's account of Jimmy Hoffa's demise published in their 2003 bestselling book titled *I Heard You Paint Houses*. Charles Brandt, a former prosecutor and author, pieces together a comprehensive narrative of the actions of Sheeran that summer day in 1975. Over a four-year period starting in 1999, Brandt recorded hours of interviews with Sheeran and in a death-bed confession admitted that he had pulled the trigger on James R. Hoffa. The time frame to kill Hoffa was developed around Bill Bufalino's daughter's wedding, which was going to take place on Friday August 1, 1975. Bill Bufalino was a Teamster lawyer and close friend of kingpin Russell Bufalino (unrelated). About 500 people from all over the country were going to attend the wedding, and it is believed that Jimmy Hoffa thought Anthony Provenzano and Russell Bufalino would be in Detroit for the nuptials, so they could meet to discuss Tony Pro's million dollar pension, as well as iron out a few things. Tony Giacalone arranged the meeting for 2:00 p.m. on Wednesday July 30, 1975, at the Red Fox Restaurant on Telegraph Avenue outside of Detroit.

According to what Sheeran told author Charles Brandt, Bufalino had given Sheeran a chance to persuade Hoffa to stop his campaign for the leadership of the Union, but his time had run out. Sheeran was driving Bufalino and their wives from Pennsylvania to the Georgiana Hotel in Detroit that Wednesday for a Friday wedding. They stopped at a restaurant outside Port Clinton, about 100 miles from Detroit, and left their wives and Bufalino's wife's older sister. A small airport was nearby, and a quick flight over the lake put Detroit about an hour away.

The way Sheeran saw it, the Mob only had two choices: murder Hoffa or put him in the plot. By doing that, they got a chance to make sure they could trust him—it was the only way. To Sheeran, Hoffa was admired, almost idolized. He did not take the order to get rid of Hoffa easily, but Sheeran figured that if he did not do it, Bufalino would get someone else and he probably would get whacked, too. Sheeran did not feel good about the assignment but he was a natural born killer. The disturbing part of the plan for Sheeran was that Hoffa could have avoided his fate anytime he wanted. All he had to do was drop out of race for the Teamster's presidency. Unfortunately for Hoffa, he believed he was untouchable.

Arriving at the small airport near Detroit, Sheeran jumped into the non-descript dusty Ford that was waiting for him. The keys were on the floor mat as planned, and he drove off to the house to meet Provenzano henchman and Local 560 business agent Salvatore "Sally Bugs" Briguglio. After driving a few minutes Sheeran pulled into the driveway behind a brown Buick. He walked up the stairs, opened the unlocked door and was greeted by Sally Bugs. From the small vestibule he could see two Italian guys sitting in the kitchen at the back of the house. They would be the cleanup crew after the deed was done. The plan was to be conducted like a military operation, which suited Sheeran to a tee. A few minutes after arriving at the brown shingled house, Jimmy Hoffa's foster son, Chuckie O'Brien, drove up. O'Brien was driving Tony Giacolone's son's maroon Mercury and the familiar car was meant to put both O'Brien and Hoffa at ease. Hoffa was expecting Tony Giacalone, so having the car, with Chuckie as the driver, was part of the bait. It was time to move. Sheeran sat in the front passenger seat with O'Brien while Sally Bugs sat in the passenger seat behind O'Brien. The maroon Mercury got to the Red Fox in less than fifteen minutes. When they got there, they saw Hoffa's green Pontiac in the restaurant's parking lot but Hoffa was nowhere in sight. O'Brien parked the car with the motor running, and a minute later they saw Hoffa coming toward his car from the area of the hard ware store behind the restaurant. O'Brien slowly pulled up to Hoffa surprising him. "What the fuck are you even doing here? Who the fuck invited you?" Hoffa screamed, poking his finger at O'Brien. Hoffa looked in the back seat and saw Sally Bugs.

"Who the fuck is he?" Hoffa yelled. "I'm with Tony Pro," Sally said. "What the fuck is going on here? Your fucking boss was supposed to be here at 2:00," Hoffa barked. Sally Bugs then pointed to the person in the front seat. Hoffa lowered his head and saw Sheeran. "His friend (Russell Bufalino) wanted to be at the thing. They're at the house waiting," Sally Bugs said. Telling Hoffa that Bufalino was going to be at meeting was the final bait. Hoffa was smart enough to know that if there was going to be any violence, Bufalino would not be there "I thought you were supposed to call me last night. I waited in front of the restaurant at 2:00 for you. You were going to be sitting in my car when they showed. I was going to make them get in for a sit-down," Hoffa said. Sheeran told Hoffa they were delayed and that Bufalino had a change of plans and wanted to meet with him at the house. Hoffa was getting really pissed off and impatient by now. About forty-five minutes had gone by since he got to the Red Fox, and he wanted to get the meeting done and over with. He then came around the car and got in and sat behind Sheeran. It worked. O'Brien took the car out of neutral and drove off. "Who the fuck is Pro sending a fucking errand boy?" Hoffa exclaimed. "We'll be there in two minutes," O'Brien piped in, trying to calm things down. Hoffa told Sheeran that he had called his wife. "You could have left a message," Hoffa said. Without missing a beat, Sheeran explained that Bufalino did not want him to say anything about the plans over the telephone. "At least somebody could've told me 2:30 . . . at the very least," Hoffa said.

The four men arrived at the house about 3:00 and stopped near the brick steps to the front door. Two cars, a brown Buick and black Ford, were in the driveway and this signaled to Hoffa that people were in the house. To Sheeran, the timing of the plot was crucial because alibis had to be considered. Hoffa got out of the rear door of the maroon Mercury while Sheeran got out of the front door at the same time. Sally Bugs then stepped out of the rear door and went around and sat in the passenger seat next to Chuckie O'Brien and they drove away. Meanwhile, Hoffa headed quickly to the steps with Sheeran behind him. Hoffa opened the front door, walked into the small vestibule while Sheeran shut the door. When Hoffa realized that nobody was coming out of any of the rooms, he knew what it was. Hoffa turned around fast, stepped around Sheeran, reaching for the doorknob. At that very moment, Sheeren fired two shots into Hoffa's head behind his right ear. Sheeran looked down the hall to make sure nobody came out to get him, then dropped the gun and walked out the door, got into his black Ford and drove back to the Pontiac airport for the short flight to Port Clinton.

Bufalino told Sheeran later that after the two Italian guys cleaned the house, they took Hoffa out the back door and put him in the trunk of the Buick. They then took Hoffa to be cremated. When that was done, the cleaners picked up Sally Bugs at Pete Vitale's meatpacking plant and drove to an airport where the three boarded a plane for New Jersey to report to Tony Pro. When Sheeran landed at the small airfield in Port Clinton, Bufalino was sleeping in Sheeran's black Lincoln. He got into his car, started the engine, and woke Bufalino from his slumber.

Bufalino looked up at Sheeran, winked at him with his good eye and in his gritty voice said, "Anyway, I hope you had a pleasant flight, my Irish friend." Sheeran looked at Bufalino, "I hope you had a good sleep." They picked up the ladies at the restaurant a few minutes later and continued their trip to Detroit, arriving just before 7:00 p.m. About six weeks after Jimmy Hoffa disappeared in 1975, a grand jury convened in Detroit. A grand jury is empowered to conduct official proceedings to investigate potential criminal conduct and determine whether criminal charges should be brought forward. Nine suspects were ordered to appear: Anthony "Tony Pro" Provenzano, Stephen Andretta, Thomas Andretta, Salvatore "Sal" Briguglio, Gabriel "Gabe" Briguglio, Francis Joseph "Frank" Sheeran, Russell Bufalino, Anthony "Tony Jack" Giacalone, and Chuckie O'Brien. All nine were represented by Bill Bufalino and all of them took the Fifth Amendment. Frank Sheeran took the Fifth on every question he was asked, including whether the prosecutor's yellow pen was yellow.

CHAPTER THIRTEEN

KUKLINSKI'S INTERVIEWS

Over the last five decades there have been numerous people coming out of the woodwork claiming they know who whacked Jimmy Hoffa. Anthony Bruno, author of The Ice Man, interviewed Richard Kuklinski in Trenton State Prison and exchanged correspondence with the contract killer. The 6'4", 300-lb Kuklinski murdered his first victim at the age of thirteen and went on to kill 100 to 250 people between 1948 to 1986. A favorite of Newark's DeCavalcante crime family and New York's Five Families, Kuklinski snuffed out his victims by every possible method. Guns, knives and his bare hands to name a few. His favorite killing method was poison cyanide. In a letter written to Anthony Bruno, Kuklinski claimed he was the one that murdered Jimmy Hoffa. Although the author does not believe Kuklinski had anything to do with Hoffa's disappearance, the letter is a stark reminder that the iconic labor leader was a tantalizing subject for a lot of malcontents who wanted a share in the mystery. In an excerpt from the letter, Kuklinski obviously refers to himself as "the big guy" and Hoffa as the "big mouth guy." Anthony Bruno believes he did this to avoid a prosecution that might have led to the death penalty. The letter is word for word, misspellings and grammatical errors included. In Kuklinski's scenario, he is in the "second car" with the "Hoboken four."

The second car with the Hoboken four in it, pull the first car over with no trouble, three men get out and take one man, a problem, out of the car big mouth guy but he soon quieted down. Tommy is driving brother Steve and Sally along with the forth big man, all know what must be done Tommy, big mouth, and Sally are in the front seat, Steve and Big Man are in the back seat. Driving down the road the big mouth guy was unconscious and Sally says our friend will be waking up soon now is a good a time as any. The Big Man took his knife and placed it on the back of big mouths neck, right were the spine meets the skull puts his left hand around the big mouths left side of his face and takes hold of the chin, presses forward with his right hand enters the neck to the throat, gurgle, gurgle it seemed like a long time but reality it wasn't. The car pulled over the big mouth guy was put in the trunk and continued the journey back to N.J.

So Kuklinski offers us another interesting explanation about what happened to Jimmy Hoffa. Is it true? It's doubtful. Given the time, the ambiguities, and the conflicting evidence in the Hoffa case, it is doubtful we will ever know the truth. That is why the answer to the question—What happened to Jimmy Hoffa?—will remain organized crime's most famous mystery.

CHAPTER FOURTEEN

CONCLUSION

There will always be a fascination with James Riddle Hoffa. In a 1994 letter to the *New York Times*, Barbara Ann Crancer, daughter of Jimmy Hoffa, wrote: *In the review of Mob Lawyer by Frank Ragano and Selwyn Raab (June 5), Robert Lacey writes, Jimmy Hoffa, Santo Trafficante and Carlos Marcello were three of the most notorious underworld figures of recent times. Mr. Lacey is attempting to rewrite history. He apparently wants the world to forget James R. Hoffa's dedication as an American labor leader for more than 40 years, as well as his widely recognized accomplishments on behalf of Teamsters and all working people in America. As the daughter of James R. Hoffa, I am appalled by this description of my father and shocked that you would publish it.*

The sentiment among family members and the Teamster rank and file still runs deep almost 40 years after Jimmy Hoffa's mysterious disappearance. James P. Hoffa, the son of the martyred father and current president of the Teamsters is a chip off the old block. He blames "Wall Street's greed, stupidity and fraud" for the nation's economic problems, ignoring the role that Big Government meddling in the economy played in inflating the mortgage market bubble. Like his father before him, James P. Hoffa doesn't mince words. During the Occupy Wall Street movement, the Teamsters were front and center. Hoffa told a crowd, "Let's take these sons of bitches out and give America back to America where we belong . . . we got to keep an eye on the battle that we face: The war on workers. And you see it everywhere, it is the Tea Party." After the event, Hoffa invoked the mother of all leftist clichés, telling ABC News that conservatives "want to roll the time clock back to about 1900." James R. Hoffa would have been proud of his son's accomplishments. Jimmy Hoffa Jr., a lawyer by training is known to have a radical streak like his father. Notwithstanding, there remains an underlying mythology that the Teamsters Union was stolen from James R. Hoffa by the Kennedys. In turn, he had his life stolen from him by the Mob. The unwritten banner reads something like this: Hoffa's son is going to redeem the Union in his name. That just might be a hard sell since the International Brotherhood of Teamsters president inherited a pedigree that the Union under his father had a steadfast relationship with the Mob. James R. Hoffa was the larger-than-life Teamster president who worked closely with figures from the crime underworld. In July of

1975, Hoffa disappeared mysteriously outside a suburban Detroit restaurant where he was planning to meet with two mobsters. His body has never been found and likely never will be. The disappearance of Teamsters Union leader Hoffa over 38 years ago remains one of America's most enduring mysteries and will continue to be a cold case in the eyes of the FBI until evidence is uncovered of what happened that fateful day.

The legendary connections to organized crime, corruption and violence is still a "monkey on the back" of the million-plus Teamster Union of truckers and blue-collar workers. For years the word Teamster was commonly perceived to be a synonym for gangster. Historian Thaddeus Russell, in his book titled *A Renegade History of the United States,* provides vivid portraits of renegades like Jimmy Hoffa. The more these accidental revolutionaries existed, resisted, and persevered, the more receptive society became to change. Thaddeus Russell likened anti-hero James R. Hoffa to General George S. Patton. He exalted bravery and despised frailty, and presented himself as the toughest, strongest, and most ruthless fighter in the Union, Russell wrote. Hoffa also once proudly proclaimed his potential to be "the meanest bastard that God ever created." James Riddle Hoffa was a working-class individual who turned the Teamsters Union into a nationwide movement before falling from grace and going to jail for racketeering. After serving almost five years in a federal prison, Hoffa was pardoned by President Richard Nixon and was attempting his comeback when he was summoned to a meeting with two Mafia dons on July 30, 1975. His abandoned car was found outside the Detroit restaurant and no trace of him has been found since. There are many theories about why the Mob wanted Hoffa dead. One of the most probable presumptions is that the Teamsters' pension was supporting the Mob's projects in Las Vegas and the Mafia was anxious that Hoffa's bid to retake the Union would lead to the money drying up. Another fascinating and haunting speculation is that Hoffa had something to do with the JFK assassination. It is believed John F. Kennedy's murder by the Mob was a way to placate Hoffa. In the early 1960s Robert Kennedy was closing in on the Union boss with racketeering charges and some within the Mafia believed Hoffa wasn't appreciative enough for the Mafia's hit on the president. Robert Kennedy relentlessly pursued Jimmy Hoffa and organized crime's influence over organized labor much of his professional career. Hoffa despised the Kennedys and the Kennedys hated Hoffa. Frank Ragano, one of Hoffa's lawyers and also the attorney for Tampa crime boss Santo Trafficante alleges that in early 1963 Hoffa begged Trafficante to kill JFK. True or not, the notion that Jimmy Hoffa had the influence to persuade the Mob to murder the President of the United States is astounding.

In Charles Brandt's book *I Heard You Paint Houses*, Frank Sheeran's death-bed confession that he killed Jimmy Hoffa is a chilling and plausible account of what happened the day of his disappearance. "Hoffa was Sheeran's friend but you didn't defy orders. If he hadn't killed him he'd have been shot himself," said Brandt. Sheeran revealed to Brandt that the mafia was upset because Hoffa hadn't shown enough gratitude over Dallas in 1963. It is rumored to this day that Lee Harvey Oswald was not alone in the assassination of JFK and that the Mob was behind the murder. In his death-bed confession Frank Sheeran admitted taking three rifles to Baltimore that would eventually end up in Dallas. With the 50th anniversary of JFK's assassination approaching, innuendos of Jimmy Hoffa'a complicity in the killing looms like a dark shadow in the life and times of the iconic labor leader. Frank Sheeran's account of his role in Jimmy Hoffa's disappearance that summer day in July of 1975 is shocking. "I know now that my father killed his friend, Jimmy," his daughter Delores said. "He had no choice, he was acting on orders. If he hadn't done it, he would have been killed." On orders of Mob boss Russel Buffalino, Sheeran told Brandt how he lured Hoffa into an empty house and shot him twice in the back of the head. A second Mafia hit squad disposed of the body. The Mob didn't need Jimmy Hoffa anymore and they simply couldn't take any chances of Hoffa regaining the Teamsters leadership. Millions of dollars were at stake . . . Hoffa didn't have a chance.

ଔ ଔ   ଔ ଔ   ଔ ଔ

ABOUT THE AUTHOR

Born in Oberlahnstein, Germany, William Hryb immigrated to Thunder Bay, Canada at a young age. Ukrainian by heritage, he is a freelance print and broadcast journalist, a member of the Professional Writers Association of Canada (PWAC), Superior Scribes, a professional Thunder Bay writer's guild. Hryb is a regular contributing writer to various trade magazines, periodicals and newspaper publications such as *Canadian Sailings Transportation & Trade Logistics, Bayview, On the Level, Cruise Ship North America*, and the *Ukrainian Weekly*. He also is the President and Managing Director of Thunder Bay Shipping, Inc.

Hryb has been associated with the marine industry since 1975, representing a word wide network of ship owners and charterers. He was appointed in 2007 by the International Joint Commission (IJC) as the Commercial

Navigation representative for Canada with the International Upper Great Lakes Study (IUGLS). The five-year study is a major bi-national examination of water level issues on the Upper Great Lakes.

Before entering the shipping industry, he studied Communication Arts, majoring in broadcast journalism. After his studies in the early 1970s he travelled extensively throughout South America as a freelance journalist. Hryb has interviewed a wide range of political and business leaders in his career, including The Right Honourable John Diefenbaker, the 13th prime minister of Canada.

Hryb is the co-author of *Movers & Mavericks*, a collection of profiles of people that lived in the Thunder Bay area over the last 100 years. Next year, *Movers & Mavericks II* will be released and later in 2014, he will co-author with Elle Andra-Warner the book about the luxury yacht *Gunilda* that sank in Lake Superior more than 100 years ago.

Since January 2011 he has been co-host and co-producer of the popular Internet radio program *Crime Beat* on the ArtistFirst World Radio Network.

BIBLIOGRAPHY

Brandt, C. 2004. *I Heard You Paint Houses*. New Hampshire: Steertforth Press.

Franco, J., & Hammer, R. 1987. *Hoffa's Man: The Rise and Fall of Jimmy Hoffa as Witnessed by His Strongest Arm*. New York: Simon and Schuster.

Harper, S. J. 2007. *Crossing Hoffa: A Teamster's Story*. Minnesota: Borealis Books.

Harrington, W. G. 1996. *Columbo: The Hoffa Connection*. New York: Forge Books.

Humphreys, Adrian. 2011. *The Weasel: A Double Life in the Mob*. New Jersey: Wiley.

Jones, C. 2006. *Hoffa'sWomen: The Slur They Made Their Banner*. North Carolina: Red Springs Publishing.

Kennedy, R. F. 1960. *The Enemy Within*. Massachusetts: DaCapo Press.

McShane, T. F. 2001. *The Death of Jimmy Hoffa*. CreateSpace Independent Publishing Platform.

Miller, F. P. (ed), Vandome, Agnes (ed), McBrewster, John (ed). 2010. *Jimmy Hoffa*. International Book Marketing Service.

Moldea, D. E. (1978). *The Hoffa Wars: Teamsters, Rebels, Politicians, and the Mob*. London: Paddington Press: distributed by Grosset & Dunlap; First edition.

Russell, T. 2001. *Out of the Jungle: Jimmy Hoffa and the Remaking of the American Working Class*. New York: Knopf; First edition.

Walsh, M. J. 2011 (10 30). Hoffa V. U. S. U.S. Supreme Court Transcript of Record with Supporting Pleadings. Gale, U.S. Supreme Court Records.

Canadian Broadcasting Corporation. June 20, 2013. "The Current" with Anna Maria Tremonti. *Jimmy Hoffa's Mysterious Disappearing Act.*

Obituary of Edgar D. Croswell, *New York Times,* November 21, 1990.

The History Channel. Biography – Jimmy Hoffa. March 19, 2012.

CURRENT AND FORTHCOMING TITLES FROM
STRATEGIC MEDIA BOOKS

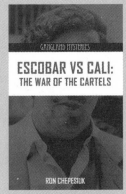

ESCOBAR VS CALI
The War of The Cartels

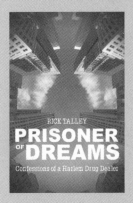

PRISONER OF DREAMS
Confessions of
a Harlem Drug Dealer

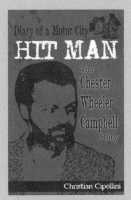

**DIARY OF A MOTOR CITY
HIT MAN**
The Chester
Wheeler Campbell Story

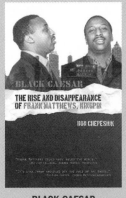

BLACK CAESAR
The Rise and Disappearance of
Frank Matthews, Kingpin

AVAILABLE FROM STRATEGICMEDIABOOKS.COM, AMAZON, AND MAJOR BOOKSTORES NEAR YOU.

COMING IN 2014

THE SICILIAN MAFIA
A True Crime Travel Guide

THE GODFATHER OF CRACK:
The True Story of Freeway Ricky Ross

LUCKY LUCIANO:
Mysterious Tales of a Gangland Legend